Overcoming Obstacles

Become Overcomers

By: Bill Vincent

© 2016 by Bill Vincent.

All rights reserved. No part of this book may be reproduced, stored in a retrieval system or transmitted in any form or by any means without the prior written permission of the publishers, except by a reviewer who may quote brief passages in a review to be printed in a newspaper, magazine or journal.

Softcover 978-1-60796-986-0

PUBLISHED BY REVIVAL WAVES OF GLORY BOOKS & PUBLISHING

www.revivalwavesofgloryministries.com

Litchfield, IL

Published in the United States of America

Table of Contents

About the Author 4
Introduction 5
The Power of the Tongue 7
Healing the Wounded 13
Overcoming Temptation 18
A Prophetic Word 25
Obedience to Pastors 28
Sin in Secret 31
Motives of the Heart 34
Turning on God 41
Satan's Cults 44
Breaking the Yoke 52
Drugs and Alcohol 57
Various Addictions 60
Our Heavenly Father 65
Seducing Spirit 67
To Be Loved and To Love God 75
The Healing Hurdle 78
Provision and the Love of Money 84
Good and Bad Fears 91
God is a Comforting God 97
Abominable Things 100
Getting Out of the Rut 102
Mindset and Limitations 103
God Will Help Us 105
New Days Ahead 107
Discovering Our Purpose 111
Removing the Obstacle 115
Recommended Books 119

About the Author

Bill Vincent is no stranger to understanding the power of God. Not only has he spent over twenty years as a Minister with a strong prophetic anointing, he is now also an Apostle and Author with Revival Waves of Glory Ministries in Litchfield, IL. Along with his wife, Tabitha, he, leads a team providing apostolic oversight in all aspects of ministry, including service, personal ministry and Godly character.

Bill offers a wide range of writings and teachings from deliverance, to experiencing presence of God and developing Apostolic cutting edge Church structure. Drawing on the power of the Holy Spirit through years of experience in Revival, Spiritual Sensitivity, and deliverance ministry, Bill now focuses mainly on pursuing the Presence of God and breaking the power of the devil off of people's lives.

His books 48 and counting has since helped many people to overcome the spirits and curses of Satan. For more information or to keep up with Bill's latest releases, please visit www.revivalwavesofgloryministries.com. To contact Bill, feel free to follow him on twitter @revivalwaves.

Introduction

This book is to help saints get through trials. We all have hard times that seem to go on and on. The anointed Word of God will help those who believe to grow instead of fall. Many Christians have given up at the brink of a miracle. One thing to understand is God has called us to be overcomers. In this we are going to reveal some obstacles that Satan wants to destroy the Saints with. We do not have to go from defeat to defeat but victory to victory.

John 16:33 These things I have spoken unto you, that in me ye might have peace. In the world ye shall have tribulation: but be of good cheer; I have overcome the world.

1 John 4:4 Ye are of God, little children, and have overcome them: because greater is he that is in you, than he that is in the world.

Through God we are able to overcome the world. Christians can have true peace. Greater is Jesus on the inside of us than the devil in the world.

Revelation 2:11 And they overcame him by the blood of the Lamb, and by the word of their testimony; and they loved not their lives unto the death.

1 John 5:4 For whatsoever is born of God overcometh the world: and this is the victory that overcometh the world, even our faith.

We are sealed by the blood of Jesus. We can overcome the works of the devil by the blood of the lamb. Testify when you overcome obstacles to encourage other Christians. When we are born again the Bible says that we overcome the world when we became born again. Through faith we are saved and through faith we can overcome obstacles.

The Power of the Tongue

This is an obstacle that everyone has been a part of. What is it about rumors, gossip and things alike, that make them so painful when we are their victims? A friend comes and tells of a report they heard and being spread among others. The report is untrue, but is still being spread. What are some things you might want to do? What do most of us usually do? Why do we seem to enjoy them so much (when we hear them) when they are about others.

A personal problem with the power of the tongue is, when we confess bad things about ourselves. It may be physically, financially and more. There is bad and good things that we can confess about our lives. The power of the tongue can altar your life. Remember you have the power to make your life change if you have been affected by the power of the tongue.

Proverbs 18:21 says, "Death and life are in the power of the tongue: and they that love it shall eat the fruit thereof."

According to the Bible, just how important are the words we speak?
Good things words can accomplish.

Proverbs 12:14 says, "A man shall be satisfied with good by the fruit of his mouth: and the recompense of a man's hands shall be rendered unto him."

Recompense means,
To make repayment compensate.

Proverbs 12:14 would say, "A man shall be satisfied with good by the fruit of his mouth: and the repayment of a man's hands shall be rendered unto him.

Remember say good things because (repayment) will be returning back to you."

Proverbs 15:23 says, "A man hath joy by the answer of his mouth: and a word spoken in due season, how good is it!"

Proverbs 24:24, 25 says, "He that saith unto the wicked, Thou art righteous; him shall the people curse, nations shall abhor him: But to them that rebuke him shall be delight, and a good blessing shall come upon them."

Abhor means,
To shrink in disgust, hatred and detest.

Proverbs 24:24, 25 would say, "He that saith unto the wicked, Thou art righteous; him shall the people curse, nations shall detest him: But to them that rebuke him shall be delight, and a good blessing shall come upon them."

Proverbs 15:1 says, "A Soft answer turneth away wrath: but grievous words stir up anger."

Grievous means,
1. Causing grief
2. Causing suffering and very serious

Proverbs 15:1 would say, "A Soft answer turneth away wrath: but (causing suffering) words stir up anger."

Proverbs 8:6, 7 says, "Hear; for I will speak of excellent things; and the opening of my lips shall be right things. For my mouth shall speak truth; and wickedness is an abomination to my lips."

Psalms 34:1 says, "I Will bless the Lord at all times: his praise shall continually be in my mouth."
Good things words can accomplish personally.

We must believe God with our words.
Hebrews 11:6 says, "But without faith it is impossible to please him: for he that cometh to God must believe that he is, and that he is a rewarder of them that diligently seek him."

We cannot stand in faith by confessing things contrary to the Word of God.

(Say things like I'm going to be healed.)

Hebrews 11:1 says, "Now faith is the substance of things hoped for, the evidence of things not seen."

Confess the word of God in your life.

Philippians 4:19 says, "But my God shall supply all your need according to his riches in glory by Christ Jesus."

Bad things words can accomplish.
Proverbs 16:8 says, "Better is a little with righteousness than great revenues without right."
This means that it is better to say a little bit of good about someone, than to say allot of bad things.

Proverbs 15:4 says, "A wholesome tongue is a tree of life: but perverseness therein is a breach in the spirit."

Perverseness means,
1. Deviating from what is considered right and good.
2. Corrupt
3. Wicked

Breach means,
1. Being broken.
2. A break in friendly relations.

Proverbs 15:4 would say, "A (pure) tongue is a tree of life: but (corrupt) therein is a (break in friendly relations) in the spirit."

Proverbs 15:18 says, "A wrathful man stirreth up strife: but he that is slow to anger appeaseth strife."

Proverbs 11:9 says, "An hypocrite with his mouth destroyeth his neighbour: but through knowledge shall the just be delivered."

Hypocrite means,
1. A fake
2. A fraud
3. A deceiver

Proverbs 11:9 would say, "An (deceiver) with his mouth destroyeth his neighbour: but through knowledge shall the just be delivered."

Proverbs 13:3 says, "He that keepeth his mouth keepeth his life: but he that openeth wide his lips shall have destruction."

I remember an old saying.....If you can't say anything good don't say anything at all.

Bad things words can accomplish personally.
People say things like I'm sick, poor, depressed and defeated. According to the Word of God that is not standing in faith.

James 1:6-8 says, "....let him ask in faith, nothing wavering. For he that wavereth is like a wave of the sea driven with the wind and tossed. For let not that man think that he shall receive any thing of the Lord. A double minded man is unstable in all his ways.
Hebrews 11:1 says, "Now faith is the substance of things hoped for, the evidence of things not seen."

This scripture is a good example....If we confess (I'm sick) all the time, we probably will remain sick according to faith in the Word of God.

Remember,
Hebrews 11:6 says, "But without faith it is impossible to please him: for he that cometh to God must believe that he is, and that he is a rewarder of them that diligently seek him."

Final wrap-up of what can happen with your words,
Proverbs 26:24-28 says, "He that hateth dissembleth with his lips, and layeth up deceit within him; When he speaketh fair, believe him not: for there are seven abominations in his heart. Whose hatred is covered by deceit, his wickedness shall be shewed before the whole congregation. Whoso diggeth a pit shall fall therein: and he that rolleth a stone, it will return upon him. A lying tongue hateth those that are afflicted by it; and a flattering mouth worketh ruin.

Three are things that eventually happen to a person who misuses words about others.
1. Exposed to others.
2. The more you say the deeper you get.
3. The words of your mouth can ruin you.

Bad things personally,
1. Confessing negative all the time will make it impossible to please God.
2. Negative confessions will hinder God from accomplishing what his Word declares.

Good words about others would result in,
Proverbs 16:24 says, "Pleasant words are as an honeycomb, sweet to the soul, and health to the bones."
Your soul will prosper and become very healthy.

Good thing personally.
1. Pleasing God through faith.

2. Stand on the Word of God will become a mountain moving faith.

Conclusion:

This week focus on care and prayer....In your work place, neighborhood, home, church, or just on the phone. You will be tempted to use evil speech instead of the wonderful healing power of good speech. Commit to one week, for using words that build up and heal only.

Stand in faith confessing the Bible. It doesn't matter what circumstances come stand on God's incorruptible Word.

If you feel you can, share the area of greatest temptation as the focus of prayer. (EVERYONE SUFFERS FROM THIS PROBLEM, SO....Don't try to tackle all of the areas at once---you'll fail for sure. Just try to get a good start at one place.

Healing the Wounded

Many people in this world have been wounded some way or another. One thing that we have to understand is that several times we don't even realize that we've been wounded. Understanding how we have been wounded is part of overcoming the wounds. When we continue on not realizing that we've been wounded usually results in more wounds. The more wounds we have the harder for us to overcome them. Through God we can be healed.

Psalms 147:3 says, "He healeth the broken in heart, and bindeth up their wounds."

Broken hearted means,
1. Crushed by sorrow, grief, or disappointment; inconsolable
Wounds means,
1. Any hurt or injury to the feelings, honor, etc.
The next verse finely declares the power of God.

Psalms 147:4 says, "He telleth the number of the stars; he calleth them all by their names."

Healing the broken in heart, and bindeth up their wounds. That the same being who spoke the worlds into existence, does in his mercy cheer the wounded, and heal the broken hearted. First, here is a great ill which is a broken heart; and secondly, a great mercy which healeth the broken heart and bindeth up their wounds. Man is a double being: he is composed of body and soul, each of the portions may receive injury of hurt. The wound of the body are extremely painful. Remember that in his mercy providing means whereby wounds may be healed and injuries repaired. Wounds are known not felt.

(Before you disagree hear us while we explain.)

You However, who have broken hearts, can no longer be used to love. We intend to help you on the important subject of broken hearts, and the great healing provided for them.

Let us figure out a broken heart. What is it? Understand that there are several kinds of broken hearts. Some are what we call naturally broken, and some are spiritually broken. There have been hearts broken by a great number. A wife has been neglected by a husband who was once totally focused on the wife in every way. Even now she tenderly loves him. Despised by the man who once showed her great affection, she has known what a broken heart is.

A friend is forsaken by one upon whom he learned, to who their very close to, so that their two hearts had grown into one; and he feels that his heart is broken, for the other half of himself is cut-off from him.

Talking about these types of situations,
(One doesn't care to be around the other as before.)
(One friend moves.)

One who we have always told our sorrows betrays our confidence; the conscience may possibly be a broken heart. When you fall in love with someone and you find has been with another results, in a severe broken heart.

It may occur when someone says something hateful to a friend or family member. Something happens to that person such as death or accident will result in, a broken heart.

A child or a parent that says I hate you can result in a broken heart.

There was a time I was supposed to stay with some family for a few days. During this time I was approx. ten years old. My mom drove to the family's house, in which the parents were not home. My mom went on home and soon after, the parents got home. There was much excitement in my heart to get to stay there. Immediately we all had to get in the car to go for a ride. One thing I remember is I recognized that we were heading toward where I lived.

We arrived in front of my house and hatefully one parent screamed get out, and then they pealed out and left. This resulted in a broken heart.

One day I was working on our automobile and I cut the top of my hand pretty bad. After a few days the pain was not there anymore. The wound remained for quite a long while. A couple of weeks later I was working on something and I ripped my hand open in the same place as before.

The wounds that are there in our hearts, need to be took care by Gods great mercy. Opening the wound is more severe than the first.

We have spoken a long time on the ill of the broken heart; our second thought will be his great mercy-"He healeth the broken heart."

Psalms 147:3 says, "He healeth the broken in heart, and bindeth up their wounds."

First He (being God) only does it. Men may try to help the suffering, they may console the afflicted and cheer the distressed, but they cannot heal the broken heart, nor bind up their wounds.

The binding of the heart is done immediately by God,

Micah 7:7 says, "Therefore I will look unto the Lord; I will wait for the God of my salvation: my God will hear me."

Then again, God only may do it. Suppose we could heal your broken heart, it would be good for nothing. I do seek the Lord that, that I may never get a broken heart healed (Hear me when I say this.) except it be God.

Truly convinced sinners would rather keep his heart broken than have it healed wrongly. I ask who are suffering, would you not rather keep your broken heart as it is, than to allow a bad physician to cure it for you, and so deceive you.

Isaiah 53:4, 5 says, "Surely he hath borne our griefs, and carried our sorrows: yet we did esteem him stricken, smitten of God, and afflicted. But he was wounded for our transgressions, he was bruised for our iniquities: the chastisement of our peace was upon him; and with his stripes we are healed."

1 Peter 2:24 says, "Who his own self bare our sins in his own body on the tree, that we, being dead to sins, should live unto righteousness: by whose stripes ye were healed."

3 John 1:2 says, "Beloved, I wish above all things that thou mayest prosper and be in health, even as thy soul prospereth."

Finally, he will do it. That is a sweet thought. "He healeth the broken heart;" He will do it. Nobody else can, nobody else may, but he will. Is your heart broken? He will heal it, he is sure to heal it; for it is written-and it can never be altered, for what was true over 2000 years ago,

is true now- "He healeth the broken heart." Did Saul of Tarsus rejoice after three days of blindness? Yes, and you shall be delivered also.

"I love thee with an everlasting love"

Yes, it is true most true neither dream nor fiction, HE HEALETH THE BROKEN HEART AND BINDETH UP THEIR WOUNDS.

Overcoming Temptation

Being tempted is something all Christians face. One thing Christians need to remember is that being tempted is not sin in itself. Jesus is one of the greatest examples on temptation. The Word of God is anointed and if we learn to stand on it every day we can overcome temptation as Jesus did. Temptation will lead to sin if we do not learn to understand what the Word of God says. The importance is great to overcome temptation. Sometimes tests will come along the line of temptation.

Genesis 3:1-13 says, "Now the serpent was more subtil than any beast of the field which the Lord God had made. And he said unto the woman, Yea, hath God said, Ye shall not eat of every tree of the garden? And the woman said unto the serpent, We may eat of the fruit of the trees of the garden: But of the fruit of the tree which is in the midst of the garden, God hath said, Ye shall not eat of it, neither shall ye touch it, lest ye die. And the serpent said unto the woman, Ye shall not surely die: For God doth know that in the day ye eat thereof, then your eyes shall be opened, and ye shall be as gods, knowing good and evil. And when the woman saw that the tree was good for food, and that it was pleasant to the eyes, and a tree to be desired to make one wise, she took of the fruit thereof, and did eat, and gave also unto her husband with her; and he did eat.

And the eyes of them both were opened, and they knew that they were naked; and they sewed fig leaves together, and made themselves aprons. And they heard the voice of the Lord God walking in the garden in the cool of the day: and Adam and his wife hid themselves from the presence of the Lord God amongst the trees of the garden. And the Lord God called unto Adam, and said unto him, where art thou?

And he said, I heard thy voice in the garden, and I was afraid, because I was naked; and I hid myself. And he said, who told thee that thou wast naked? Hast thou eaten of the tree, whereof I commanded thee that thou shouldest not eat? And the man said, The woman whom thou gavest to be with me, she gave me of the tree, and I did eat. And the Lord God said unto the woman, What is this that thou hast done? And the woman said, The serpent beguiled me, and I did eat." **The devil comes to tempt us with what will separate us from God. God tells us one thing in his Word....the devil will tempt us, to get us to turn our back on God.**

Matthew 4:1-11 says, "Then was Jesus led up of the Spirit into the wilderness to be tempted of the devil. And when he had fasted forty days and forty nights, he was afterward an hungred. And when the tempter came to him, he said, If thou be the Son of God, command that these stones be made bread. But he answered and said, It is written, Man shall not live by bread alone, but by every word that proceedeth out of the mouth of God. Then the devil taketh him up into the holy city, and setteth him on a pinnacle of the temple, And saith unto him, If thou be the Son of God, cast thyself down: for it is written, He shall give his angels charge concerning thee: and in their hands they shall bear thee up, lest at any time thou dash thy foot against a stone. Jesus said unto him, It is written again, Thou shalt not tempt the Lord thy God. Again, the devil taketh him up into an exceeding high mountain, and sheweth him all the kingdoms of the world, and the glory of them; And saith unto him, All these things will I give thee, if thou wilt fall down and worship me. Then saith Jesus unto him, Get thee hence, Satan: for it is written, Thou shalt worship the Lord thy God, and him only shalt thou serve. Then the devil leaveth him, and, behold, angels came and ministered unto him."

Be like Jesus when the enemy comes to tempt you. Satan will come to tempt us at our weakest moments. This passage of scripture is something all Christians should read over and over again.

Matthew 26:41 says, "Watch and pray, that ye enter not into temptation: the spirit indeed is willing, but the flesh is weak."

Mark 14:38 says, "Watch ye and pray, lest ye enter into temptation. The spirit truly is ready, but the flesh is weak."

All who believe in God need to stand on God's Word? We need to pray concerning temptation because our flesh is weak.

Luke 8:13, 14 says, "They on the rock are they, which, when they hear, receive the word with joy; and these have no root, which for a while believe, and in time of temptation fall away. And that which fell among thorns are they, which, when they have heard, go forth, and are choked with cares and riches and pleasures of this life, and bring no fruit to perfection."

There was a time in my life that I smoked cigarettes. I quit after many years of smoking and deceiving people about it. Afterward I would be tempted to smoke. It was like a torture on the inside. This is hard to explain how difficult it was to overcome that temptation. Through God's Word, prayer and falling away from that flesh desire of smoking.

Romans 6:12-14 says, "Let not sin therefore reign in your mortal body, that ye should obey it in the lusts thereof. Neither yield ye your members as instruments of unrighteousness unto sin: but yield yourselves unto God, as those that are alive from the dead, and your members as instruments of righteousness unto God. For sin shall not have dominion over you: for ye are not under the law, but under grace."

Romans 12:21 says, "Be not overcome of evil, but overcome evil with good."

When temptation comes we need to understand that it will try to overtake us. Use Romans 12:21 as I believe it says in other words, do not allow evil to overcome you, but overcome evil with the things of God.

1 Corinthians 7:5 says, "Defraud ye not one the other, except it be with consent for a time, that ye may give yourselves to fasting and prayer; and come together again, that Satan tempt you not for your incontinency."

This is so important. Being tempted is a tremendous thing for us to go through. This scripture says to fast and pray. It is my belief to use each of these different passages concerning fasting.

1 Corinthians 8:9-13 says, "But take heed lest by any means this liberty of yours become a stumbling block to them that are weak. For if any man see thee which hast knowledge sit at meat in the idol's temple, shall not the conscience of him which is weak be emboldened to eat those things which are offered to idols; And through thy knowledge shall the weak brother perish, for whom Christ died? But when ye sin so against the brethren, and wound their weak conscience, ye sin against Christ. Wherefore, if meat make my brother to offend, I will eat no flesh while the world standeth, lest I make my brother to offend."

Ephesians 6:10-18 says, "Finally, my brethren, be strong in the Lord, and in the power of his might. Put on the whole armour of God, that ye may be able to stand against the wiles of the devil. For we wrestle not against flesh and blood, but against principalities, against powers, against the rulers of the darkness of this world, against spiritual wickedness in high places. Wherefore take unto you the whole armour of God, that ye may be able to withstand in the evil day, and having done all, to stand. Stand therefore, having your loins girt about with truth, and having on the breastplate of righteousness; And your feet shod with the preparation of the gospel of peace; Above all, taking the shield of faith, wherewith ye shall be able to quench all the fiery darts of the wicked. And take the helmet of salvation, and the sword of the Spirit, which is the word of God: Praying always with all prayer and supplication in the Spirit, and watching thereunto with all perseverance and supplication for all saints."

All through the Word of God we are made aware of how to be equipped through Christ. Use this passage to put on your whole armor.

1 Peter 1:6, 7 says, "Wherein ye greatly rejoice, though now for a season, if need be, ye are in heaviness through manifold temptations:

That the trial of your faith, being much more precious than of gold that perisheth, though it be tried with fire, might be found unto praise and honour and glory at the appearing of Jesus Christ."

Matthew 6:9-13 says, "After this manner therefore pray ye: Our Father which art in heaven, Hallowed be thy name. Thy kingdom come. Thy will be done in earth, as it is in heaven. Give us this day our daily bread. And forgive us our debts, as we forgive our debtors. **And lead us not into temptation**, but deliver us from evil: For thine is the kingdom, and the power, and the glory, for ever. Amen.

Pray this prayer or something similar. It is important to keep our prayer life up at all times.

Luke 22:40 says, "And when he was at the place, he said unto them, Pray that ye enter not into temptation."

Now is the time to change your time with God to a daily more intimate relationship. Recognize when you are most tempted. Stand even in you weakest moments.

Pray that you are not led into temptation. Fast as you seek God concerning the days ahead.

Here are a few scripture that I keep before me. I believe the Word of God is truth. When temptation comes I use these scriptures to help me overcome.

1 John 4:4 says, "Ye are of God, little children, and have overcome them: because greater is he that is in you, than he that is in the world."

James 4:7 says, "Submit yourselves therefore to God. Resist the devil, and he will flee from you."

James 1:12-16 says, "Blessed is the man that endureth temptation: for when he is tried, he shall receive the crown of life, which the Lord hath promised to them that love him. Let no man say when he is tempted, I am tempted of God: for God cannot be tempted with evil, neither tempteth he any man: But every man is tempted, when he is drawn away of his own lust, and enticed. Then when lust hath conceived, it bringeth forth sin: and sin, when it is finished, bringeth forth death. Do not err, my beloved brethren."

Being tempted is not sin. If we give into temptation, that is sin.
Hebrews 2:18 says, "For in that he himself hath suffered being tempted, he is able to succour them that are tempted."

Hebrews 4:15 says, "For we have not an high priest which cannot be touched with the feeling of our infirmities; but was in all points tempted like as we are, yet without sin."

1 Corinthians 10:13 says, "There hath no temptation taken you but such as is common to man: but God is faithful, **who will not suffer you to be tempted above that ye are able; but will with the temptation also make a way to escape, that ye may be able to bear it.**"

You will not be tempted more than you are able to stand through. Remember there will be a way to escape. You also will be able to bear it.

A Prophetic Word

One or more people may single you out and speak God's Word over you. This topic can be hard to understand. I believe God wants you to overcome whatever may block you from receiving the Prophetic Word.

The Prophet's role is based on,
Deuteronomy 18:18 says, "I will raise them up a Prophet from among their brethren, like unto thee, and will put my words in his mouth; and he shall speak unto them all that I shall command him."

In the New Testament times the gift of prophecy continued with people who now had the outpouring of the Holy Spirit.

1 Timothy 1:18 says, "This charge I commit unto thee, son Timothy, according to the prophecies which went before on thee, that thou by them mightest war a good warfare."

1 Timothy 4:14 says, "Neglect not the gift that is in thee, (by the Holy Spirit) which was given thee by prophecy, with the laying on of the hands of the presbytery."

Prophetic today,
The Holy Spirit still uses people to declare the Word of the Lord. God can use anyone in the prophetic. Those who minister need to fast, pray and flow in the Holy Spirit. Usually those who have the Gift of prophecy are anointed in that area.

1 Corinthians 12:7-11 says, "But the manifestation of the Spirit is given to every man to profit withal. For to one is

given by the Spirit the word of wisdom; to another the word of knowledge by the same Spirit;

To another faith by the same Spirit; to another the gifts of healing by the same Spirit; To another the working of miracles; to another prophecy; to another discerning of spirits; to another divers kinds of tongues; to another the interpretation of tongues: But all these worketh that one and the selfsame Spirit, dividing to every man severally as he will."

The ministry of the Prophet is to preach with revealed knowledge truth of God's Word. The gift of prophecy will operate in their ministry.

The gift of prophecy is a fabulous relating of God. It is exciting when God speaks personally to show that he cares. God speaking through someone that does not know what God is saying is the wonderful Word of God.

Receiving a Prophetic Word,
We must have confidence in the calling and anointing of the person delivering the word. If we don't know the person we still need to recognize the gift is of God. We can know this by the inward witness. If there is not trust in the minister you won't receive the word.

The word spoken must be spoken in front of witnesses to be judged. If someone wants to give you a word in private I'd question the word. When I have a Word of the Lord I make sure there is a leader (such as a Pastor) present. There will be less room for error.

A true Word of God will correct without condemning. Prophesy will exhort, edify, and encourage while it gives correction. to them which are in Christ Jesus, who walk not after the flesh, but after the Spirit."

The Word must line up with the Bible.

If it does not line up with God's Word it is not accurate.
1st=When you receive a Word of God Remember these few but important rules I live by.

2nd=Have confidence in the anointing of the person delivering the Word.

3rd=The word is spoken in front of witnesses to be judged.

4th=When the Word corrects it will not condemn.

5th=The Word must line up with the God's Word. (The Bible)

Obedience to Pastors

This is a difficult subject to explain but it is vital to understand. Sometimes it is hard to walk in Godly obedience. To obey your Pastor is important in this Army of God. The Pastor's are Leaders to guide us in this life of war between the things of God and Satan. We need to overcome this major obstacle no matter how much it is against our flesh.

Hebrews 13:17 says, "Obey them that have the rule over you, and submit yourselves: for they watch for your souls, as they that must give account, that they may do it with joy, and not with grief: for that is unprofitable for you."

Many Christians have found it hard to believe that this was even in the Bible. We must have someone over us and walk in obedience. Those who believe this still find it hard to follow 100%.
There have been too many churches split or damaged because of this topic.

Christians walking in disobedience or being rebellious

When we explain this topic it is only including those Pastors who are walking upright with God. If a Pastor is in a substantial sin (such as fornication) they would not be included. The Pastor that takes you down a road that is not biblical he/or/she would also not be included. Please understand that God has the answer to who to follow. It is time for all believers to pray who they are to sit under. Christians need to get out of the so called baby Christian syndrome. If you get offended by a Pastor the problem may be you not them.

(Please: If you are offended or disagree please pray and seek God, before you harden your heart along this topic.)

In this Scripture the Greek translation means to guide, as well as to rule.

Hebrews 13:17 says, "**Obey them that have the rule over you**, and submit yourselves: for they watch for your souls, as they that must give account, that they may do it with joy, and not with grief: for that is unprofitable for you."

In this scripture it talks about those who Guide and have fed the flock. (Being the Pastor)

Hebrews 13:7 says, "Remember them which have the rule over you, **who have spoken unto you the word of God**: whose faith follow, considering the end of their conversation."

I do not want to disagree nor debate church government. This is only to help those who have the problems with leaders. These things need to be overcome.

What are the Pastors supposed to do, to entitle them to obedience?
1. To go before the flock.
2. To guide them in all truth and holiness.
3. To feed them with words on eternal life.
4. Teach them all the essential doctrines.
5. To show them how to amend what is amiss.
6. Training them into outward holiness, And so much more.

The Pastors are supposed to watch over you. "Watch over your souls" as they give account.

When you read this remember disobedience is sin. Sin separates us from God. Do you apply it to yourself? Are

you growing in God within a church or not? Do you consider the importance that it deserves? When you look at the scriptures receive them as a command by God.

Hebrews 13:17 says, "Obey them that have the rule over you, and submit yourselves: for they watch for your souls, as they that must give account, that they may do it with joy, and not with grief: for that is unprofitable for you."

Hebrews 13:7 says, "Remember them which have the rule over you, who have spoken unto you the word of God: whose faith follow, considering the end of their conversation."

Sin in Secret

Sin is difficult enough but, secret sin is dangerous. Sin in secret usually would prevent us from going to Heaven. Exposing sin may be necessary if need be. God is the judge but sin definitely separates us from God. We will never be what God wants us to be living with secret sins.

Psalms 19:12 says, "Who can understand his errors? **cleanse thou me from secret faults."**

Secret sin is a result from pride and ignorance of God's law. Those with secret sin are foolish to think that they are righteous. God's Word declares that we are to bring every thought to the obedience of Christ.

2 Corinthians 10:2-6 says, "But I beseech you, that I may not be bold when I am present with that confidence, wherewith I think to be bold against some, which think of us as if we walked according to the flesh. But I beseech you, that I may not be bold when I am present with that confidence, wherewith I think to be bold against some, which think of us as if we walked according to the flesh. For though we walk in the flesh, we do not war after the flesh: (For the weapons of our warfare are not carnal, but mighty through God to the pulling down of strong holds;) Casting down imaginations, and every high thing that exalteth itself against the knowledge of God, and **bringing into captivity every thought to the obedience of Christ;** And having in a readiness to revenge all disobedience, when your obedience is fulfilled.

Sometimes secret sin can be hidden so deep. We might have sin that we do not know on the surface. The more we grow in God the more I believe that the sin that is in secret will come to the surface.

I am talking about when Christians are sinning in secret, but on the outside appear holy. The sin even leaders may have. Hiding sin from other Christians to protect their position in the Church, will result in destruction.

Psalms 90:8 says, "Thou hast set our iniquities before thee, our secret sins in the light of thy countenance."

Ecclesiastics 12:13 says, "Let us hear the conclusion of the whole matter: Fear God, and keep his commandments: for this is the whole duty of man. For God shall bring every work into judgment, with every secret thing, whether it be good or whether it be evil."

Understand that it doesn't matter whether it is good or bad. There will be judgment of every secret thing.

John 7:4 says, "For there is no man that doeth any thing in secret, and he himself seeketh to be known openly. If thou do these things, shew thyself to the world."

2 Corinthians 4:2 says, "But have renounced the hidden things of dishonesty, not walking in craftiness, nor handling the word of God deceitfully; but by manifestation of the truth commending ourselves to every man's conscience in the sight of God."

When sin is hidden it may carry with it many other sins. It may even be one or more of these sins,
1. Dishonesty
2. Craftiness or deceit

There was a time when I was young in the Lord. It seemed like every person I worked with smoked and so did I. The only place I smoked was at work. No matter what I did not want anyone to know even my girlfriend at

the time. So I would lie and deceive to hide the smoking. Using allot of cologne and candy to hide the smell as well. The feeling on the inside was horrible. One day I prayed and asked God to do what ever he had to do to deliver me do it now. God came through I was exposed to my girlfriend and truly delivered. There have not been any cigarettes since.

A secret sin is a danger regardless of the size. God's Word says,

Exodus 20:16 says, **"Thou shalt not bear false witness against thy neighbour."**

This is a form of hiding sin. Lying or to bare false witness means,
1. To make a statement that one knows is false.
2. With intent to deceive to make such statements habitually.
3. To give a false impression; deceive one! Statistics can lie.
4. A false statement or action, esp. one made with intent to deceive.

There is a hell and lying may send you there. Read Exodus 20:16 and these definitions and think for a minute. Keeping a sin in secret for what ever reason is definitely a form of lying. God will expose those.....He does in his own way.

Walk as a true Christian, transparent and righteous before God. Please do not allow any sin especially secret sin in your life. Remember Jesus will never leave you nor forsake you.

Motives of the Heart

There is attitude in many Christians. This refers to the heart. Sometime we walk along with wrong motives. One thing God is good and faithful. How do Christians really act? This is the type of Motives of the heart that have to be overcome.

Romans 4:17-22 says, "(As it is written, I have made thee a father of many nations,) before him whom he believed, even God, who quickeneth the dead, and calleth those things which be not as though they were. Who against hope believed in hope, that he might become the father of many nations; according to that which was spoken, So shall thy seed be. And being not weak in faith, he considered not his own body now dead, when he was about an hundred years old, neither yet the deadness of Sara's womb:

He staggered not at the promise of God through unbelief; but was strong in faith, giving glory to God; And being fully **persuaded** that, what he had promised, he was able also to perform."

God's Word says that we are persuaded but, we keep trying to persuade God. God is able to do what he has said he will do. Whether it be prophecy or the Bible, God will do it in his time. Doubt and unbelief will stop what God is going to do. This is one reason why we have to be fully persuaded.

James 1:2 says, "My brethren, count it all joy when ye fall into divers temptations; Knowing this, that the trying of your faith worketh patience. But let patience have her perfect work, that ye may be perfect and entire, wanting nothing. If any of you lack wisdom, let him ask of God, that giveth to all men liberally, and upbraideth not; and it shall be given him.

But let him ask in faith, nothing wavering. For he that wavereth is like a wave of the sea driven with the wind and tossed. For let not that man think that he shall receive any thing of the Lord. A double minded man is unstable in all his ways."

Sometimes we get into a situation and don't know what to do.

James 1:5 says, "If any of you lack wisdom, let him ask of God, that giveth to all men liberally, and upbraideth not; and it shall be given him."

There are three types of Christians,
1. Those that jump out ahead of God.
2. Those that don't move at all.
3. Those who hear God speak and they move when God says move.

Ephesians 4:4-10 says, "There is one body, and one Spirit, even as ye are called in one hope of your calling; One Lord, one faith, one baptism, One God and Father of all, who is above all, and through all, and in you all. But unto every one of us is given grace according to the measure of the gift of Christ. Wherefore he saith, When he ascended up on high, he led captivity captive, and gave gifts unto men. (Now that he ascended, what is it but that he also descended first into the lower parts of the earth? He that descended is the same also that ascended up far above all heavens, that he might fill all things.)

Ephesians 4:11-16 says, "And he gave some, apostles; and some, prophets; and some, evangelists; and some, pastors and teachers; For the perfecting of the saints, for the work of the ministry, for the edifying of the body of Christ:

Till we all come in the unity of the faith, and of the knowledge of the Son of God, unto a perfect man, unto the measure of the stature of the fullness of Christ: That we henceforth be no more children, tossed to and fro, and carried about with every wind of doctrine, by the sleight of men, and cunning craftiness, whereby they lie in wait to deceive; But speaking the truth in love, may grow up into him in all things, which is the head, even Christ: From whom the whole body fitly joined together and compacted by that which every joint supplieth, according to the effectual working in the measure of every part, maketh increase of the body unto the edifying of itself in love."

What is the motive of your heart is the question we will get to.
What are the reason and/or **Motive** you're a Christian. Is the reason for you not escaping hell but loving God?

If we really love God we would try to walk upright, all the days of our life.

Women say things like "you wouldn't do that if you love me." This is similar to what I'm trying to say. Love God with all your heart and be as good as you can be.

Deuteronomy 6:5 says, "And thou shalt love the Lord thy God with all thine heart, and with all thy soul, and with all thy might."

Proverbs 8:17 says, "I love them that love me; and those that seek me early shall find me."

What is the motive of your heart?
We have the, I want attitude. God wants us to walk in a real love relationship with him. Our motive is wrong when we intend to please just us and not God. Christians sometimes are so selfish. God loves you.

John 3:16-17 says, "For God so loved the world, that he gave his only begotten Son, that whosoever believeth in him should not perish, but have everlasting life. For God sent not his Son into the world to condemn the world; but that the world through him might be saved."

Some People have sat in our service and during time of prophetic ministry they would leave. These people came back about an hour later. Then they ran up to receive prophetic ministering. What is the motive of their heart? During that service I had a serious knee injury. We ministered a total of four hours. Why you may ask, the love of God. During this service there was a couple that worked in the service and turned down ministering. These are good examples of the types of motives. We as Christians should know what is right and wrong motives. I was in a meeting one time were the speaker had three altar calls. The first altar call was for a deliverance and casting out devils anointing. Three people responded to that call. Another call was for being used in the prophetic. In this call only two people responded. The last altar call was for being used in healing and miracles. The altar was full end to end.

God has called many to be in a deliverance ministry. The Word of God says that we are to seek first to prophesy. God wants you to accomplish all you are ordained to do.

God wants you to prosper and to be healed.

Ephesians 3:20,21 says, "Now unto him that is able to do exceeding abundantly above all that we ask or think, according to the power that worketh in us, Unto him be glory in the church by Christ Jesus throughout all ages, world without end. Amen."

God is able. Let's purify our motives. Love God and walk in his leading and guiding. With God we all can have true motive of the heart.

I don't watch sports or do any thing except the ministry. My walk daily is as a witness, Evangelist, prophetic minister, writing and preparing for the days ahead. Of course there is daily study and prayer to God. Showing love that I believe is the most important thing.

2 Corinthians 5:17 says, "Therefore if any man be in Christ, he is a new creature: old things are passed away; behold, all things are **become** new."

This word become is not instant but continual. This meaning God continues to renew us.

THE BIG QUESTIONS,
1. What is the reason you go to church?
2. Is God pleased with you?

(When you do anything check yourself first.)

What is the intent of your heart?
1 Corinthians 14:1-6 says, **"Follow after charity, and desire spiritual gifts, but rather that ye may prophesy**. For he that speaketh in an unknown tongue speaketh not unto men, but unto God: for no man understandeth him; howbeit in the spirit he speaketh mysteries. But he that prophesieth speaketh unto men to edification, and exhortation, and comfort. He that speaketh in an unknown tongue edifieth himself; but he that prophesieth edifieth the church. I would that ye all spake with tongues; but rather that ye prophesied: for greater is he that prophesieth than he that speaketh with tongues, except he interpret, that the church may receive edifying."

Charity is love. I believe we should desire to be a gift in the church through the Holy Spirit.
Change your motives through the anointing of God. Pray and seek God concerning your motives.

1 Corinthians 2:9-15 says, "But as it is written, Eye hath not seen, nor ear heard, neither have entered into the heart of man, the things which God hath prepared for them that love him. But God hath revealed them unto us by his Spirit: for

the Spirit searcheth all things, yea, the deep things of God. For what man knoweth the things of a man, save the spirit of man which is in him? even so the things of God knoweth no man, but the Spirit of God. Now we have received, not the spirit of the world, but the spirit which is of God; that we might know the things that are freely given to us of God. Which things also we speak, not in the words which man's wisdom teacheth, but which the Holy Ghost teacheth; comparing spiritual things with spiritual. But the natural man receiveth not the things of the Spirit of God: for they are foolishness unto him: neither can he know them, because they are spiritually discerned. But he that is spiritual judgeth all things, yet he himself is judged of no man."

1 Corinthians 2:16 says, "For who hath known the mind of the Lord, that he may instruct him? But we have the mind of Christ."
1 Corinthians 2:14 But the natural man receiveth not the things of the Spirit of God: for they are foolishness unto him: neither can he know them, because they are spiritually discerned.

This verse shows the source of wrong motive. Jesus is the source by the Holy Spirit to be the right motive.

Mark 11:22-24 says, "And Jesus answering saith unto them, Have **faith in God**. For verily I say unto you, That **whosoever** shall say unto this mountain, Be thou removed, and be thou cast into the sea; and shall not doubt in his heart, but shall believe that those things which he saith shall come to pass; he shall have whatsoever he saith. Therefore I say unto you, What things soever ye desire, when ye pray, believe that ye receive them, and ye shall have them."

Have faith in God translated from the Greek is have faith of God. This means God's faith and ability operating through you. Whosoever are you. Get this in your heart.

Mark 11:25-26 says, "And when ye stand praying, forgive, if ye have ought against any: that your Father also which is in heaven may forgive you your trespasses. But if ye do not forgive, neither will your Father which is in heaven forgive your trespasses."

Walk in forgiveness in the continual relation of this passage. It says that we have the power faith of God but we also need to walk in forgiveness.

All Christians in some way or another need help in this area of the motive of the heart. God will do it if you believe. This can be the root of other sinful things.

Turning on God

Have you turned your back on God? Is your heart right with God? The topic is backsliding. Whether you're saved, lukewarm or unsaved this chapter is for you. It is very important that we all understand what God's word says. Jesus will return for the church soon and we must be ready.

Backslider means, to slide backward in morals or religious enthusiasm; become less virtuous, less pious, etc.
The backslider needs forgiveness, God's forgiveness, man's forgiveness and forgiveness of self.

It is a serious offense to follow Jesus and then to turn to Satan's side. God does not take it lightly.

Hebrews 10:38 says, "Now the just shall live by faith: but **if any man draw back, my soul shall have no pleasure in him.**"

Luke 9:62 says, "And Jesus said unto him, No man, having put his hand to the plough, and looking back, is fit for the kingdom of God."

God's mercy always allows a space for repentance.

Repentance means, a repenting or being penitent; feeling of sorrow, etc., esp. for wrongdoing; compunction; contrition; remorse (Asking Jesus to forgive sin or wrong doing.)

Although King David committed adultery he truly repented and confessed to God. He would have been subject to the law. God's word says, "No adulterer or murderer shall inherit the kingdom of God. Judas repented to men instead of God. The Bible says that Jesus is the way to heaven.

Isaiah 55:7 says, "Let the wicked forsake his way, and the unrighteous man his thoughts: and let him return unto the Lord, and he will have mercy upon him; and to our God, for he will abundantly pardon."

Hebrews 7:25 says, "Wherefore he is able also to save them to the uttermost that come unto God by him, seeing he ever liveth to make intercession for them."

2 Peter 3:9 says, "The Lord is not slack concerning his promise, as some men count slackness; but is longsuffering to us-ward, not willing that any should perish but that all should come to repentance."

Jeremiah 3:22 says, "Return, ye backsliding children, and I will heal your backslidings. Behold, we come unto thee; for thou art the Lord our God."

If you have turned away from God, now is your chance to make your heart right before God. It doesn't matter whether you turned your heart or turned your back on God. This step is important that everyone must take to have assurance to heaven. It is time to be convinced that you are a lost sinner. Believe that Christ died for you. Believe that God will forgive you of your sins. Finally receive Jesus as your personal savior.

Pray this prayer and mean it with all your heart. Dear Jesus, I believe that you are the son of God and that you died for me and arose again on the third day. Have mercy on me. I Acknowledge and repent for my transgressions, for it was against thee that I sinned. I am truly sorry and I claim the blood for the cleansing of my iniquity. Create in me a clean heart and renew a right spirit within me. Help me to overcome, never again to follow the enticements of the devil. Please come into my

heart this day. I sincerely want to be thy child. Thank you Jesus for saving me Amen!

Welcome to the family of God!!

Satan's Cults

We need to understand Satan is the instigator of all opposition to God and is the power behind all cults. Many people have been led wrong by several cults. Sometimes cults mix the gospel with the lies of the devil. This is something that even Christians can fall into. We are talking about obstacles that will control the lives of people. Cults are usually very zealous people that try to win people to their belief. Allot of cults in America go door to door and we need to be ready.

The devil let pride come in when he said "I will be the most high."

Ezekiel 28:13 says, "Thou hast been in Eden the garden of God; every precious stone was thy covering, the sardius, topaz, and the diamond, the Beryl, the onyx, and the jasper, the sapphire, the emerald, and the carbuncle, and gold: the workmanship of thy tabrets and of thy pipes was prepared in thee **in the day that thou wast created."**

1 Peter 5:8 says, "Be sober, be vigilant; because **your adversary the devil**, as a roaring lion, walketh about, seeking whom he may devour:"

Adversary means, A person who opposes or fights against another; opponent; enemy of or characterized by opposing parties,
SYNONYM: OPPONENT

The Adversary Satan

(God loves all people and so should we. The false religion that is against God is what we all need to overcome.)

We need to know what a cult is,
1. A system of religious worship or ritual
2. A quasi-religious group, often living in a colony, with a charismatic leader who indoctrinates members with unorthodox or extremist views, practices, or beliefs.
3. Devoted attachment to, or extravagant admiration for, a person, principle, or lifestyle, esp. when regarded as a fad! The cult of nudism"
4. The object of such attachment
5. A group of followers; sect

Some Christians are afraid of even the names devil and Satan.

The devil has created new religions and/or cults with their false teachers and prophets. This is to keep people in spiritual darkness and bondage.

2 Corinthians 4:4 says, "In whom the god of this world hath blinded the minds of them which believe not, lest the light of the glorious gospel of Christ, who is the image of God, should shine unto them."

John 14:6 says, "Jesus saith unto him, I am the way, the truth, and the life: no man cometh unto the Father, but by me."

Deuteronomy 18:10-12 says, "There shall not be found among you any one that maketh his son or his daughter to pass through the fire, or that **useth divination, or an observer of times, or an enchanter, or a witch. Or a charmer, or a consulter with familiar spirits, or a wizard, or a necromancer**. For all that do these things are an **abomination unto the Lord**: and because of these

abominations the Lord thy God doth drive them out from before thee."

These are things that are of the devil,
1. (Ouija boards) this is more than a game. I have played this so called game. After a few times I thought other people were moving it. When I was young I played this game and when we were done playing, a part of the game began to move. It spelled out deadly evil things. There were times I asked things that were a lie and it answered by spelling out this is not true. That day I knew it was evil and I never allowed it within my midst again.
2. **Wizard = (A psychic)** on who supposedly communicates with spirits. Psychic means, (Of or having to do with the psyche, or mind....A person who is supposedly sensitive to forces beyond the physical world....A spiritualistic medium.) The TV has live psychics on all the time. The bible indicates that psychics are of the devil.

Deuteronomy 18:10-12 says, "There shall not be found among you any one that maketh his son or his daughter to pass through the fire, or that **useth divination, or an observer of times, or an enchanter, or a witch. Or a charmer, or a consulter with familiar spirits, or a wizard, or a necromancer**. For all that do these things are an **abomination unto the Lord**: and because of these **abominations** the Lord thy God doth drive them out from before thee."

One time in a true prophetic church service there was a woman, I'll never forget. The woman was sick physically and was really depressed. The prophet of God called her out and spoke to her about all she was going through. The last thing God said was that she was calling psychics all the time and it was going to kill her if she didn't quit. God also said that after she quit, she would be totally healed within one year. Many years after that I saw her and she looked different. I had the privilege to talk with her and she said she was healed. PRAISE GOD!!!

Psychics are destroying people's lives. The Word of God says "my people parish because of lack of knowledge." Psychics tell people who they are going to marry. That marriage is dammed.

3. (Horoscopes) this is something most people have tried and even joked about. No matter what <u>I believe that according to God....this also is of the devil.</u> Before you read one more, realize that you are opening yourself to wrong spirits.

4. (Dungeons and Dragons) One day as a teen I was asked to play this so called board Game. We began to play and with minutes I felt an ire feeling. It was a role playing kind of game. One of the players acted violent and I quit and left. This same boy was really addicted to this game.

There was a day on the bus on the way home from school. This boy was sweating and shaking. I asked him what was wrong and he said tomorrow my dad is going to beat up my best friend. He also said that it was because of that game! The next day I was walking to the bus stop. When I got there the boy's dad came and beat this boy to the point that he could hardly move. (This is a true story) Approximately five or so years later, I saw that boy. He looked like he was dressed for Halloween. I'm not talking about the clothes but the countenance. There was a real dark look in his eyes.

5. (Mormons) Known as The Church Of Latter Day Saints. Here is a list of things they teach,

A. The universe is governed by a head god head and his council. Together they thought up creating the earth and man.

B. God has wives.

C. God has a physical body and he can't be in more than one place at a time.

D. There are many Gods.

E. Jesus and Satan are brothers.

F. Mary was not a virgin.

G. Jesus was married.

H. We can also become gods.

I. The black race is cursed.

J. The Bible is incomplete and has a lot of errors in translation.
K. Joseph Smith was a holy prophet and prophets are above scripture.
L. Joseph Smith is our final Judge.
This is all contrary to the Word of God. (THE BIBLE)
6. (Jehovah Witness)

Here is what the Jehovah Witness believe about God,
A. God's personal name is Jehovah.
B. Only Jehovah is from everlasting to everlasting.
C. The Holy Spirit is a force not a person.
D. Satan originated the Trinity doctrine.
E. Aloha is the plural of majesty and does not mean he was a triune being.
F. He lives on Pleiades. (in space somewhere)

Here is what the Jehovah Witness believe about Jesus,
A. He was a creation of God and did not pre-exist with God.
John 1:1 says, "In the beginning was the Word, and the Word was with God, and the Word was God."
B. Originally Jesus was the arch angel Michael and he was changed into the mortal man, Jesus.
C. He was born October 1, in 2 BC of the Virgin Mary.
D. He humbled himself to die on a torture stake. God raised him as a spirit and gave him immortality and he became an immortal version of Michael the angel.
E. His resurrected body was only spirit not flesh.
G. Charles Take Russell wrote "the man Jesus is dead forever dead"

Here is what the Jehovah Witness believe about the Holy Spirit,
A. He is an invisible force but not part of the trinity.

Here is what the Jehovah Witness believe about salvation,
A. Adam is not included in the ransomed because he forfeited his chance.
B. His perfect human life was laid down in death, but not for sin and punishment.

C. All who are faithful to do God's will and carry out their dedication will receive everlasting life.
D. Only 144,000 get to go to heaven, everyone else that receives eternal life gets to stay on the earth down here.
E. "It is a gross twisting of the scriptures to throw Jesus' words of John 3:3 to make them embrace all of mankind.
John 3:3 says, "Jesus answered and said unto him, Verily, verily, I say unto thee, Except a man be born again, he cannot see the kingdom of God."

Here is what the Jehovah Witness believe about Hell,
A. The doctrine of a burning hell cannot be real.
This is all contrary to the Word of God. (THE BIBLE)
If you disagree with anything within this chapter, please pray and seek God. Read these scriptures to come to your conclusion and understanding.

Isaiah 9:6 says, "For unto us a child is born, unto us a son is given: and the government shall be upon his shoulder: and his name shall be called Wonderful, Counselor, The mighty God, the everlasting Father, The Prince of Peace."

JESUS

Hebrews 9:27 says, "And as it is appointed unto men once to die, but after this the judgment."

Luke 16:22,23 says, "And it came to pass, that the beggar died, and was carried by the angels into Abraham's bosom: **the rich man also died, and was buried; And in hell he lift up his eyes, being in torments**, and seethe Abraham afar off, and Lazarus in his bosom."

If we are fooled by Satan's Cults, we will be buried in torment.

Matthew 24:5 says, "For many shall come in my name, saying, I am Christ; and shall deceive many."

Matthew 24:24 says, "For there shall arise false Christ's, and false prophets, and shall shew great signs and wonders; insomuch that, if it were possible, they shall deceive the very elect."

John 10:9 says, "I am the door: by me if any man enter in, he shall be saved, and shall go in and out, and find pasture."

Philippians 4:13 says, "I can do all things through Christ which strengthened me."

1 John 4:4 says, "Ye are of God, little children, and have overcome them: because greater is he (being Jesus)that is in you, than he(being Satan) that is in the world."

Discontinue any participation of any cult products. Make sure there is nothing that you possess of any relation to cults.

2 Corinthians 6:7 says, "By the word of truth, by the power of God, by the armour of righteousness on the right hand and on the left."

Ephesians 6:10-12 says, "Finally, my brethren, be strong in the Lord, and in the power of his might. Put on the whole armour of God, that ye may be able to stand against the wiles of the devil. For we wrestle not against flesh and blood, but against principalities, against powers, against the rulers of the darkness of this world, against spiritual wickedness in high places."

Ephesians 6:18 says, "Praying always with all prayer and supplication in the Spirit, and watching thereunto with all perseverance and supplication for all saints."

Revelation 12:11 says, "And they overcame him by the blood of the Lamb, and by the word of their testimony; and they loved not their lives unto the death."

This is an obstacle all the people in the world face in different ways. Satan is behind many religions. No matter what.....please stay close to God and stay led by God. Have this information near your front door for answers to questions you can ask. Even having facts before you the cults may agree with you but, don't allow yourself to be persuaded to the right nor the left.

Breaking the Yoke
(The Anointing)

The anointing of the Holy Spirit is very important. The anointing is what breaks the yoke of bondage. It is hard enough to get through life in this day. We need the anointing along with God the Father, God the Son and the Holy Spirit. Many Christians are in bondage and the way to overcome is, with the anointing through the Holy Spirit.

2 Corinthians 3:4 says, "And such trust have we through Christ to God-ward."
You cannot make it without God. This is not talking about salvation. It's talking about the anointing. We can understand the Word of God completely. The anointing is the power when you pray.

1 John 2:26-29 says, "These things have I written unto you concerning them that seduce you. But the anointing which ye have received of him abideth in you, and ye need not that any man teach you: but as the same anointing teacheth you of all things, and is truth, and is no lie, and even as it hath taught you, ye shall abide in him. And now, little children, abide in him; that, when he shall appear, we may have confidence, and not be ashamed before him at his coming. If ye know that he is righteous, ye know that every one that doeth righteousness is born of him."

There is an anointing that is available through the Holy Spirit. We need the power of the Holy Spirit.

Have you ever had something in your life that is holding you back?

Isaiah 10:27 says, "And it shall come to pass in that day, that his burden shall be taken away from off thy shoulder, and his yoke from off thy neck, and **the yoke shall be destroyed because of the anointing."**

The letter killeth but the anointing giveth life. The Bible without the anointing is just words.

All of us have some area in our life that is hindering our walk with Jesus. They have to be broken with the anointing. The anointing breaks the yoke of bondage.

Hosea 4:6 says, "My people are destroyed for lack of knowledge: because thou hast rejected knowledge, I will also reject thee, that thou shalt be no priest to me: seeing thou hast forgotten the law of thy God, I will also forget thy children."

The devil robs the saints when we are not aware. The anointing helps us to be ready and aware.

1 Corinthians 12:1-7 "Now concerning spiritual gifts, brethren, I would not have you ignorant. Ye know that ye were Gentiles, carried away unto these dumb idols, even as ye were led. Wherefore I give you to understand, that no man speaking by the Spirit of God calleth Jesus accursed: and that no man can say that Jesus is the Lord, but by the Holy Ghost. Now there are diversities of gifts, but the same Spirit. And there are differences of administrations, but the same Lord. And there are diversities of operations, but it is the same God which worketh all in all. But the manifestation of the **Spirit is given to <u>every man </u>to profit withal**."

1 Corinthians 12:8 says, "For to one is given by the Spirit the word of wisdom; to another the word of knowledge by the same Spirit." The anointing and gifts are to be in operation in the church, in these last days. We put the responsibility within the five fold ministry. It said every man, meaning to move in the anointing through the Holy Spirit.

There have been a large number of people that we have had the opportunity to minister to. Different things like, addictions, drugs, alcohol, sinful nature, marriages and women that have been abused. The anointing of Jesus Christ is the power that does the work. The anointing makes the difference.

The anointing comes when we believe and humbly ask God for it. We need to be prayed up and in God's Word. There are a large number of things that the anointing comes for. Here are just a few things,
1. in Evangelism.
2. as moms and dads.
3. in marriages.
4. Prayer for children.
5. Ministering from the pulpit.

Remember, the anointing is of God. The power is of God. This means the glory is Gods and his only. We have to be humble because we are flesh and of sin. God is the only source of the works.

1 Corinthians 14:1-7 says, "Follow after charity, and desire spiritual gifts, but rather that ye may prophesy. For he that speaketh in an unknown tongue speaketh not unto men, but unto God: for no man understandeth him; howbeit in the spirit he speaketh mysteries. But he that prophesieth speaketh unto men to edification, and exhortation, and comfort. He that speaketh in an unknown tongue edifieth himself; but he that prophesieth edifieth the church. I would that ye all spake with tongues; but rather that ye prophesied: for greater is he that prophesieth than he that speaketh with tongues, except he interpret, that the church may receive edifying. Now, brethren, if I come unto you speaking with tongues, what shall I profit you, except I shall speak to you either by revelation, or by knowledge, or by prophesying, or by doctrine? And even things without life giving sound, whether pipe or harp, except they give a distinction in the sounds, how shall it be known what is piped or harped?"

The gift of prophecy is becoming more and more in these last days. I believe that we all need to know God's voice by hearing, seeing (much like a vision), dreams and feelings. There is coming a time were we all minister one to another.

1 Corinthians 2:9-12 says, "But as it is written, Eye hath not seen, nor ear heard, neither have entered into the heart of man, the things which God hath prepared for them that love him. But God hath revealed them unto us by his Spirit: for the Spirit searcheth all things, yea, the deep things of God. For what man knoweth the things of a man, save the spirit of man which is in him? even so the things of God knoweth no man, but the Spirit of God. Now we have received, not the spirit of the world, but the spirit which is of God; that we might know the things that are freely given to us of God."

1 Corinthians 2:13-16 says, "Which things also we speak, not in the words which man's wisdom teacheth, but which the Holy Ghost teacheth; comparing spiritual things with spiritual. But the natural man receiveth not the things of the Spirit of God: for they are foolishness unto him: neither can he know them, because they are spiritually discerned. But he that is spiritual judgeth all things, yet he himself is judged of no man. For who hath known the mind of the Lord, that he may instruct him? But we have the mind of Christ."

Read these verses again,
1 Corinthians 2:9 says, "But as it is written, Eye hath not seen, nor ear heard, neither have entered into the heart of man, the things which God hath prepared for them that love him."

1 Corinthians 2:14 says, "But the natural man receiveth not the things of the Spirit of God: for they are foolishness unto him: neither can he know them, because they are spiritually discerned."

Draw near to God and he will draw near to us. If we are going to be effective we need the anointing to break any power of the enemy. There was a man at a nursing home that would play the piano for us. God moved me by the anointing to minister to him. God showed me that there was something out of alignment. I began to tell him what God said, and I asked him if I laid my hands on him would he be healed. He said yes. After kneeling down by where he was sitting I lifted his legs up. We checked the length and found that one leg was approximately 3/4 of an Inch short. The prayer started for the anointing to heal this problem. It took a few minutes but we kept praying and then God made him whole. Both legs were now the same PRAISE GOD!! This man said that he had back trouble for years and I could understand why.

The power of the anointing is something to covet.

Romans 8:29-32 says, "For whom he did foreknow, he also did predestinate to be conformed to the image of his Son, that he might be the firstborn among many brethren. Moreover whom he did predestinate, them he also called: and whom he called, them he also justified: and whom he justified, them he also glorified. What shall we then say to these things? If God be for us, who can be against us? He that spared not his own Son, but delivered him up for us all, how shall he not with him also freely give us all things?"

Ecclesiastes 3:11 says, "**He hath made every thing beautiful in his time:** also he hath set the world in their heart, so that no man can find out the work that God maketh from the beginning to the end."

May you be anointed to be the man or woman of God you are ordained to be. May you find the yoke of bondage broken by our almighty God?

Drugs and Alcohol

This topic is a deep subject. Before you skip through this chapter, listen to us for a minute. Drugs and alcohol may be affecting you or someone close to you. With God this obstacle can be removed.

There was a time in my life; I thought that I couldn't live without drugs and alcohol. God moved on me and saved me from sin, drugs and alcohol.

Acts 3:19 says, "Repent ye therefore, and be converted, that your sins may be blotted out, when the times of refreshing shall come from the presence of the Lord."

Isaiah 1:18 says, "Come now, and let us reason together, saith the Lord: though your sins be as scarlet, they shall be as white as snow; though they be red like crimson, they shall be as wool."

Romans 10:13 says, "For whosoever shall call upon the name of the Lord shall be saved."

1 John 1:9 says, "If we confess our sins, he is faithful and just to forgive us our sins, and to cleanse us from all unrighteousness."

2 Corinthians 5:17 says, "Therefore if any man be in Christ, he is a new creature: old things are passed away; behold, all things are become new."

John 8:36 says, "If the Son therefore shall make you free, ye shall be free indeed."

Romans 12:1says, "I beseech you therefore, brethren, by the mercies of God, that ye present your bodies a living sacrifice, holy, acceptable unto God, which is your reasonable service."

James 4:7 says, "Submit yourselves therefore to God. Resist the devil, and he will flee from you."

Romans 13:14 says, "But put ye on the Lord Jesus Christ, and make not provision for the flesh, to fulfil the lusts thereof."

One thing we always say is that we believe the Word of God. God's Word is being revealed and it will set you free in Jesus name. If you want God to mean business with you.....you must mean business with him.

In your walk with Jesus, determine to never let Satan rob you. Here are thoughts to obedience of Christ.

1 Corinthians 6:20 says, "For ye are bought with a price: therefore glorify God in your body, and in your spirit, which are God's."

Colossians 3:17 says, "And whatsoever ye do in word or deed, do all in the name of the Lord Jesus, giving thanks to God and the Father by him."

Your body is to be pure and holy

Ephesians 5:18 says, "And be not drunk with wine, wherein is excess; but be filled with the Spirit."

In the past decade we have had the opportunity to minister to homeless people. These people are often referred to as winos. Alcohol has destroyed homes and lives a great deal. People will slowly kill their selves. Understand that God's word was sent to me an alcoholic and drug attic. God totally delivered me from even the temptation. If you know of others that have a similar problem, do not cram the gospel down their throat. Prayer works wonders walking in love toward them.

Various Addictions

This is for all of us that think we are just fine. Addictions are of many fields of life. Addictions are set to hold you captive this is why; we need to overcome this obstacle.

Addict means, a person with a **strong habit** with a drug.

Habit means, involuntary pattern of behavior acquired by frequent repetition.

Habit Synonyms, usage, routine, compulsion, use, want **addictions.**

Jeremiah 13:23 says, "Can the Ethiopian change his skin, or the leopard his spots? then may ye also do good, that are accustomed to do evil."

Jeremiah 22:21 says, "I spake unto thee in thy prosperity; but thou saidst, I will not hear. This hath been thy manner from thy youth, that thou obeyedst not my voice."

Micah 2:1 says, "Woe to them that devise iniquity, and work evil upon their beds! when the morning is light, they practise it, because it is in the power of their hand."

It means you are a work alcoholic.....when someone always puts work first. Work always comes before food, family and their own life.

Deuteronomy 4:9 says, "Only take heed to thyself, and keep thy soul diligently, lest thou forget the things which thine eyes have seen, and lest they depart from thy heart all the days of thy life: but teach them thy sons, and thy sons' sons."

Psalms 22:6 says, "But I am a worm, and no man; a reproach of men, and despised of the people."

Here are some things that are the parent's job concerning addictions,
Teach,
Deuteronomy 6:7 says, "And thou shalt teach them diligently unto thy children, and shalt talk of them when thou sittest in thine house, and when thou walkest by the way, and when thou liest down, and when thou risest up."

Train,
Proverbs 22:6 says, "Train up a child in the way he should go: and when he is old, he will not depart from it."

Provide for,
2 Corinthians 12:14 says, "Behold, the third time I am ready to come to you; and I will not be burdensome to you: for I seek not yours, but you: for the children ought not to lay up for the parents, but the parents for the children."

To nurture,
Ephesians 6:4 says, "And, ye fathers, provoke not your children to wrath: but bring them up in the nurture and admonition of the Lord."
To control,
1 Timothy 3:4 says, "One that ruleth well his own house, having his children in subjection with all gravity."

To love,
Titus 2:4 says, "That they may teach the young women to be sober, to love their husbands, to love their children."

Husband's responsibilities,
Ephesians 5:25 says, "Husbands, love your wives, even as Christ also loved the church, and gave himself for it."

1 Peter 3:7 says, "Likewise, ye husbands, dwell with them according to knowledge, giving honour unto the wife, as unto

the weaker vessel, and as being heirs together of the grace of life; that your prayers be not hindered."

Wives responsibilities,
Ephesians 5:22 says "Wives, submit yourselves unto your own husbands, as unto the Lord."

1 Timothy 3:11 says, "Even so must their wives be grave, not slanderers, sober, faithful in all things."

1 Peter 3:1 says, "Likewise, ye wives, be in subjection to your own husbands; that, if any obey not the word, they also may without the word be won by the conversation of the wives."

The home is very important for our attention.

2 Corinthians 7:1 says, "Having therefore these promises, dearly beloved, let us cleanse ourselves from all filthiness of the flesh and spirit, perfecting holiness in the fear of God."

Different addictions may be.....Smoking, drinking caffeine and drugs. There has been health drugs, prescription drugs and over the counter energy pills.

There was a time I played sports in school. A few people were taking an over the counter energy pill. A close friend was taking twice what was indicated on the bottle. One day we were playing basketball and he fell to the ground at age 16 and died of a heart attack.

1 Corinthians 3:16 says, "Know ye not that ye are the temple of God, and that the Spirit of God dwelleth in you."

1 Corinthians 6:19 says, "What? know ye not that your body is the temple of the Holy Ghost which is in you, which ye have of God, and ye are not your own."

2 Corinthians 6:16 says, "And what agreement hath the temple of God with idols? for ye are the temple of the living God; as God hath said, I will dwell in them, and walk in them; and I will be their God, and they shall be my people."

Another great addiction is computers and/or Internet. Some people have four or more e-mail addresses that take all of their time. Just to check four e-mails can take hours. There is even more time. Searching, downloading and updating are a great amount of time. (I exclude anyone who does computer/Internet work for God) Check out this suggested log out,
8:00 A.M. Get up.
8:15 A.M. Check e-mails.
9:00 A.M. Get ready for work.
Go to work.
5:00 P.M. Get home.
6:00 P.M. Supper.
7:00 P.M. Check e-mail and more.
10:00 P.M. Go to bed.

If this chart is even close you are addicted. It is about time to let God set you free.

Psalms 69:13 says, "But as for me, my prayer is unto thee, O Lord, in an acceptable time: O God, in the multitude of thy mercy hear me, in the truth of thy salvation."

Isaiah 49:8 says, "Thus saith the Lord, In an acceptable time have I heard thee, and in a day of salvation have I helped thee: and I will preserve thee, and give thee for a covenant of the people, to establish the earth, to cause to inherit the desolate heritages."

Any time that I have spent any amount of time doing something, God has brought me to correction. I played games on the computer more that I should have. There was a time I had to watch every Baseball, Basketball, Football and Hockey game of my favorite team.

Something to keep in mind is, as long as what you do does not take you away from God it may be OK. "To him that knoweth to do good and doeth it not to him it is sin." God will show what is right in your life. You have to decide to have God in his fullness or the addictions. The more we receive of God the more that is required. You can overcome any and all addictions.

Our Heavenly Father

In this chapter I want to talk about God and the relationship He wants to have with us. And about the love of God and the joy he wants us to have. This is an obstacle with all Christians alike.

Years ago I had a wrong concept of God. I Thought God was mean--trying to make my life miserable. It wasn't God.....it was the things of life, Satan's attacks, me because I didn't seek God first before I chose to do certain things.
God's will is not to make us miserable, but for us to know Him as, a Father. Some people are blessed with good parents....I was. Others weren't as blessed as I was. Maybe it was hard for some of you to have a good relationship with one or both of your parents. If you haven't had a good father or a good relationship with your earthly father, it may be difficult for you to have the kind of relationship with God that He desires.

Have you gone through things in life that caused you pain or sorrow? So many Christians have had so much emotional pain. Bad marriage or loved someone that broke your heart. Loss of loved one....someone died that you dearly loved and it has left a void or an empty place in your heart. I have experienced these sorrows. I went through pain for years after the death of my dad when I was six years of age.

(Remember divorce is able to be forgiven of.)

God wants to fill these voids that have been left in us. When God takes away something-He fills with something good. God is loving and kind and merciful. We are human and we make mistakes. God is forgiving and wants to help us have better lives; to be happy, to love us, and to heal us-- emotionally and physically.

God wants to replace the sorrow and pain with joy.

1 Chronicles 16:27 says, "Glory and honour are in his presence; strength and gladness are in his place."

Psalms 126:5 says, "They that sow in tears shall reap in joy."

God wants to release us from the pain and sorrow that we sometimes have and to give us joy in its place. Don't allow yourselves to live the rest of your lives with pain and heartbreak inside. Ask the Lord to set you free from it and to give you joy and gladness in its place. **He CAN** and will do this for you. Cry out from your heart and ask Him now to heal you emotionally. **Right now where you are, Let us bow our heads right now and ask our Father in heaven to set us free from our hurts, our sorrow, and our pain for whatever the reason.**

Seducing Spirit

This is something that all Churches and the Body of Christ need to be aware of. A seducing spirit may come through an individual or even a group of people. It becomes a personal attachment to transferring its wrath through the Church. Results can be destructive; controlling, seductive, manipulative, wrecking marriages and so much more. Some people get along with some and not others. This can be a result of a seducing spirit.

1 Corinthians 15:33 says, "Be not deceived: evil communications corrupt good manners."

Proverbs 13:20 says, "He that walketh with wise men shall be wise: but a companion of fools shall be destroyed."

A strong transferring of spirits
1 John 4:4 says, "Ye are of God, little children, and have overcome them: because greater is he that is in you, than he that is in the world."

1 Corinthians 2:12-14 says, "Now we have received, not the spirit of the world, but the spirit which is of God; that we might know the things that are freely given to us of God. Which things also we speak, not in the words which man's wisdom teacheth, but which the Holy Ghost teacheth; comparing spiritual things with spiritual. But the natural man receiveth not the things of the Spirit of God: for they are foolishness unto him: neither can he know them, because they are spiritually discerned."

James 1:5 says, "If any of you lack wisdom, let him ask of God, that giveth to all men liberally, and upbraideth not; and it shall be given him."

We as God's children need to walk together.

Amos 3:3 says, "Can two walk together, except they be agreed?"

We need to keep the Word of God within us during this day we are living in....Talking about reading the Word daily and sitting under others as they teach and preach the Word. Armed and ready for the seducing spirits and alike.

Ephesians 6:11, 12 says, "Put on the whole armour of God, that ye may be able to stand against the wiles of the devil. For we wrestle not against flesh and blood, but against principalities, against powers, against the rulers of the darkness of this world, against spiritual wickedness in high places."

1 Corinthians 15:33, 34 says, "Be not deceived: evil communications corrupt good manners. Awake to righteousness, and sin not; for some have not the knowledge of God: I speak this to your shame."

1 Corinthians 16:14-18 says, "Let all your things be done with charity. I beseech you, brethren, (ye know the house of Stephanas, that it is the firstfruits of Achaia, and that they have addicted themselves to the ministry of the saints,) That ye submit yourselves unto such, and to every one that helpeth with us, and laboureth. I am glad of the coming of Stephanas and Fortunatus and Achaicus: for that which was lacking on your part they have supplied. For they have refreshed my spirit and yours: therefore acknowledge ye them that are such."

Come out from among them and be ye separate. God's word indicates that we are to be separate from doing what is contrary to His Word. There can be a transferring of spirits, just by being around wrong spirits.

Deuteronomy 20:8 says "And the officers shall speak further unto the people, and they shall say, What man is there that is fearful and fainthearted? let him go and return unto his house, lest his brethren's heart faint as well as his heart."

A great number of other things that a seducing spirit can be related are.....Bringing division, discord, disunity, strife, complaining, murmuring and even religious spirits. (These things take place in the Church.)

2 Thessalonians 2:11, 12 says, "And for this cause God shall send them strong delusion, that they should believe a lie: That they all might be damned who believed not the truth, but had pleasure in unrighteousness."

Only by staying filled with the Spirit of God can we withstand the powerful attacks of Satan. The Spirit of a man or woman will eventually receive whichever spirit he or she is in the company of. Here is three different types' human spirits, the Spirit of God and the spirit of this world.

1 Corinthians 2:11, 12 says, "For what man knoweth the things of a man, save the spirit of man which is in him? even so the things of God knoweth no man, but the Spirit of God. Now we have received, not the spirit of the world, but the spirit which is of God; that we might know the things that are freely given to us of God."

All Christians sometimes want to live both worlds. The Spirit we yield to will dominate our spirit.

Romans 6:13-16 says, "Neither yield ye your members as instruments of unrighteousness unto sin: but yield yourselves unto God, as those that are alive from the dead, and your members as instruments of righteousness unto God. For sin shall not have dominion over you: for ye are not under the law, but under grace. What then? shall we sin, because we are not under the law, but under grace? God forbid. Know ye not, that to whom ye yield yourselves servants to obey, his servants ye are to whom ye obey; whether of sin unto death, or of obedience unto righteousness?"

Matthew 6:24 says "No man can serve two masters: for either he will hate the one, and love the other; or else he will hold to the one, and despise the other. Ye cannot serve God and mammon."

Psalms 1:1says, "Blessed is the man that walketh not in the counsel of the ungodly, nor standeth in the way of sinners, nor sitteth in the seat of the scornful."

Those who associate with unsaved and get married is a source of becoming spiritually dead according to Romans 8:6-8

Romans 8:6-8 says, "For to be carnally minded is death; but to be spiritually minded is life and peace. Because the carnal mind is enmity against God: for it is not subject to the law of God, neither indeed can be. So then they that are in the flesh cannot please God."

Ephesians 4:22-27 says, "That ye put off concerning the former conversation the old man, which is corrupt according to the deceitful lusts; And be renewed in the spirit of your mind; And that ye put on the new man, which after God is created in righteousness and true holiness. Wherefore putting away lying, speak every man truth with his neighbour: for we are members one of another. Be ye angry, and sin not: let not the sun go down upon your wrath: Neither give place to the devil.

1 Peter 5:8 says, "Be sober, be vigilant; because your adversary the devil, as a roaring lion, walketh about, seeking whom he may devour:"

Generation curses in my opinion are related to a seducing spirit.

Exodus 20:5 says, "Thou shalt not bow down thyself to them, nor serve them: for I the Lord thy God am a jealous God, visiting the iniquity of the fathers upon the children unto the third and fourth generation of them that hate me;"

Leaders need to understand that seducing spirits are vital to comprehend.

Hebrews 13:17 says, "Obey them that have the rule over you, and submit yourselves: for they watch for your souls, as they that must give account, that they may do it with joy, and not with grief: for that is unprofitable for you."

2 Kings 2:9, 10 says, "And it came to pass, when they were gone over, that Elijah said unto Elisha, Ask what I shall do for thee, before I be taken away from thee. And Elisha said, I pray thee, let a double portion of thy spirit be upon me. 10. And he said, Thou hast asked a hard thing: nevertheless, if thou see me when I am taken from thee, it shall be so unto thee; but if not, it shall not be so."

2 Kings 2:11-13 says, "And it came to pass, as they still went on, and talked, that, behold, there appeared a chariot of fire, and horses of fire, and parted them both asunder; and Elijah went up by a whirlwind into heaven. And Elisha saw it, and he cried, My father, my father, the chariot of Israel, and the horsemen thereof. And he saw him no more: and he took hold of his own clothes, and rent them in two pieces. He took up also the mantle of Elijah that fell from him, and went back, and stood by the bank of Jordan;"

Philippians 2:19-22 says, "But I trust in the Lord Jesus to send Timotheus shortly unto you, that I also may be of good comfort, when I know your state. For I have no man likeminded, who will naturally care for your state. For all seek their own, not the things which are Jesus Christ's. But ye know the proof of him, that, as a son with the father, he hath served with me in the gospel."

Matthew 12:25 says, "And Jesus knew their thoughts, and said unto them, Every kingdom divided against itself is brought to desolation; and every city or house divided against itself shall not stand:"

1 Corinthians 12:4, 5 says, "Now there are diversities of gifts, but the same Spirit. And there are differences of administrations, but the same Lord."
Make sure in your walk with God, you consider who you sit under. We need to sit under someone preaching the true Word of God. Any time the doctrine they teach is contrary; on an ongoing basis.....We must discontinue sitting there.

2 Corinthians 11:3, 4 says, "But I fear, lest by any means, as the serpent beguiled Eve through his subtilty, so your minds should be corrupted from the simplicity that is in Christ. For if he that cometh preacheth another Jesus, whom we have not preached, or if ye receive another spirit, which ye have not received, or another gospel, which ye have not accepted, ye might well bear with him."

Galatians 5:9 says, "A little leaven leaveneth the whole lump."

Luke 12:15 says, "And he said unto them, Take heed, and beware of covetousness: for a man's life consisteth not in the abundance of the things which he possesseth."

Begin to know that your leaders are true of God. Recognize whether their fruit is good. Study God's Word to know true doctrine.

1 Corinthians 3:13-15 says, "Every man's work shall be made manifest: for the day shall declare it, because it shall be revealed by fire; and the fire shall try every man's work of what sort it is. If any man's work abide which he hath built thereupon, he shall receive a reward. If any man's work shall be burned, he shall suffer loss: but he himself shall be saved; yet so as by fire."

Numbers 22:6 says, "Come now therefore, I pray thee, curse me this people; for they are too mighty for me: peradventure I shall prevail, that we may smite them, and that I may drive them out of the land: for I wot that he whom thou blessest is blessed, and he whom thou cursest is cursed."

1 Thessalonians 5:12 says, "And we beseech you, brethren, to know them which labour among you, and are over you in the Lord, and admonish you;"

Ecclesiastes 10:8 says, "He that diggeth a pit shall fall into it; and whoso breaketh an hedge, a serpent shall bite him. Whoso removeth stones shall be hurt therewith; and he that cleaveth wood shall be endangered thereby."

Numbers 33:52-56 says, "Then ye shall drive out all the inhabitants of the land from before you, and destroy all their pictures, and destroy all their molten images, and quite pluck down all their high places: And ye shall dispossess the inhabitants of the land, and dwell therein: for I have given you the land to possess it. And ye shall divide the land by lot for an inheritance among your families: and to the more ye shall give the more inheritance, and to the fewer ye shall give the less inheritance: every man's inheritance shall be in the place where his lot falleth; according to the tribes of your fathers ye shall inherit. But if ye will not drive out the inhabitants of the land from before you; then it shall come to pass, that those which ye let remain of them shall be pricks in your eyes, and thorns in your sides, and shall vex you in the land wherein ye dwell. Moreover it shall come to pass, that I shall do unto you, as I thought to do unto them."

1 John 5:18 says, "We know that whosoever is born of God sinneth not; but he that is begotten of God keepeth himself, and that wicked one toucheth him not."

Deuteronomy 4:15-17 says, "Take ye therefore good heed unto yourselves; for ye saw no manner of similitude on the day that the Lord spake unto you in Horeb out of the midst of the fire: Lest ye corrupt yourselves, and make you a graven image, the similitude of any figure, the likeness of male or female, The likeness of any beast that is on the earth, the likeness of any winged fowl that flieth in the air,"

Deuteronomy4:18, 19 says, "The likeness of any thing that creepeth on the ground, the likeness of any fish that is in the waters beneath the earth: And lest thou lift up thine eyes unto heaven, and when thou seest the sun, and the moon, and the stars, even all the host of heaven, shouldest be driven to worship them, and serve them, which the Lord thy God hath divided unto all nations under the whole heaven."

The job as a leader is to equip the Saints, to watch and see the enemy's tactics.

Ezekiel 3:17 says, "Son of man, I have made thee a watchman unto the house of Israel: therefore hear the word at my mouth, and give them warning from me."

Ezekiel 3:21says, "Nevertheless if thou warn the righteous man, that the righteous sin not, and he doth not sin, he shall surely live, because he is warned; also thou hast delivered thy soul."

We hope that leaders and Saints alike can use this topic to understand and be ready for seducing spirits etc.

To Be Loved and To Love God

You may ask the question.....How could love be an obstacle? It is that sometimes because of our past, we may not understand love. It's time for us to know that God loves us and that we love Him according to the Word of God.

Jude 1:2 says, "Mercy unto you, and peace, and love, be multiplied."

Mercy means, Grace, kindness, forgiveness, pity, charity (love), sympathy and compassion.

Psalms 103:1-5 says, "Bless the Lord, O my soul: and all that is within me, bless his holy name. Bless the Lord, O my soul, and forget not all his benefits: Who forgiveth all thine iniquities; who healeth all thy diseases; Who redeemeth thy life from destruction; who crowneth thee with lovingkindness and tender mercies; Who satisfieth thy mouth with good things; so that thy youth is renewed like the eagle's."

The Great love of God.
Deuteronomy 7:13-15 says, "And he will love thee, and bless thee, and multiply thee: he will also bless the fruit of thy womb, and the fruit of thy land, thy corn, and thy wine, and thine oil, the increase of thy kine, and the flocks of thy sheep, in the land which he sware unto thy fathers to give thee. Thou shalt be blessed above all people: there shall not be male or female barren among you, or among your cattle. And the Lord will take away from thee all sickness, and will put none of the evil diseases of Egypt, which thou knowest, upon thee; but will lay them upon all them that hate thee."

John 3:16, 17 says, "For God so loved the world, that he gave his only begotten Son, that whosoever believeth in him should not perish, but have everlasting life. For God sent not his Son into the world to condemn the world; but that the world through him might be saved."

Sin means, a) An offense against God, religion, or good morals *b*) the condition of being guilty of continued offense against God, religion, or good morals.

Saved means, *Theol.* to deliver from sin and its penalties.

John 14:13-16 says, "And whatsoever ye shall ask in my name, that will I do, that the Father may be glorified in the Son. If ye shall ask any thing in my name, I will do it. If ye love me, keep my commandments. And I will pray the Father, and he shall give you another Comforter, that he may abide with you for ever;"

John 14:26,27 says, "But the Comforter, which is the Holy Ghost, whom the Father will send in my name, he shall teach you all things, and bring all things to your remembrance, whatsoever I have said unto you. Peace I leave with you, my peace I give unto you: not as the world giveth, give I unto you. Let not your heart be troubled, neither let it be afraid."

Proverbs 8:17 says, "I love them that love me; and those that seek me early shall find me."

God does love you very much. There was a time in my life, God healed me. One arm was shorter than the other and it grew out. I backslid afterward and completely turned my back on God. When God reached out to me, I came back to God. One day I checked the length of my arms and realized that Satan stole my healing. I prayed and ask God to give me my healing and told God how sorry I was. Soon after I came to realize that God healed me again.

Psalms 37:4, 5 says, "Delight thyself also in the Lord: and he shall give thee the desires of thine heart. Commit thy way unto the Lord; trust also in him; and he shall bring it to pass."

Deuteronomy 6:5 says, "And thou shalt love the Lord thy God with all thine heart, and with all thy soul, and with all thy might."

Revelation 2:1-7 says, "Unto the angel of the church of Ephesus write; These things saith he that holdeth the seven stars in his right hand, who walketh in the midst of the seven golden candlesticks; I know thy works, and thy labour, and thy patience, and how thou canst not bear them which are evil: and thou hast tried them which say they are apostles, and are not, and hast found them liars: And hast borne, and hast patience, and for my name's sake hast laboured, and hast not fainted. Nevertheless I have somewhat against thee, because thou hast left thy first love. Remember therefore from whence thou art fallen, and repent, and do the first works; or else I will come unto thee quickly, and will remove thy candlestick out of his place, except thou repent. But this thou hast, that thou hatest the deeds of the Nicolaitans, which I also hate. He that hath an ear, let him hear what the Spirit saith unto the churches; To him that overcometh will I give to eat of the tree of life, which is in the midst of the paradise of God." Keeping your first love for God is important. Do you remember falling in love and all you thought about was that special someone. Loving God should be our number 1 priority.

Deuteronomy 11:1 says, "Therefore thou shalt love the Lord thy God, and keep his charge, and his statutes, and his judgments, and his commandments, alway."

God loves us so much that he sent his only son to die. It is time to make our priorities straight to love God also.....With all our heart.

The Healing Hurdle

I was taught that God put sickness on us and we would only be healed if it be God's will. Using the incorruptible Word of God, I learned that what I believed was contrary to God. This is an obstacle that all saints face in some facet.

Exodus 15:26 says, "And said, If thou wilt diligently hearken to the voice of the Lord thy God, and wilt do that which is right in his sight, and wilt give ear to his commandments, and keep all his statutes, I will put none of these diseases upon thee, which I have brought upon the Egyptians: for I am the Lord that healeth thee."

Isaiah 45:7 says, "I form the light, and create darkness: I make peace, and create evil: I the Lord do all these things."

Micah 1:12 says, "For the inhabitant of Maroth waited carefully for good: but evil came down from the Lord unto the gate of Jerusalem."

These are scriptures some try to use to convince us something is out of context. God did not create sin or sickness for Christians to struggle with. This is a result of man's disobedience. The devil is the source of evil and sickness.

Acts 10:38 says, "How God anointed Jesus of Nazareth with the Holy Ghost and with power: who went about doing good, and healing all that were oppressed of the devil; for God was with him."

Jesus is our healer.....God is not going around putting sickness on people. Jesus overcame sin, sickness and death. Now we can overcome also.

Romans 8:2 says, "For the law of the Spirit of life in Christ Jesus hath made me free from the law of sin and death."

Revelation 20:10 says, "And the devil that deceived them was cast into the lake of fire and brimstone, where the beast and the false prophet are, and shall be tormented day and night for ever and ever."

If it be God's will he will heal me.

2 Peter 3:9 says, "The Lord is not slack concerning his promise, as some men count slackness; but is longsuffering to us-ward, not willing that any should perish but that all should come to repentance."

Revelation 22:17 says, "And the Spirit and the bride say, Come. And let him that heareth say, Come. And let him that is athirst come. And whosoever will, let him take the water of life freely."

Isaiah 53:4, 5 says, "Surely he hath borne our griefs, and carried our sorrows: yet we did esteem him stricken, smitten of God, and afflicted. But he was wounded for our transgressions, he was bruised for our iniquities: the chastisement of our peace was upon him; and with his stripes we are healed."

Matthew 8:17 says, "That it might be fulfilled which was spoken by Esaias the prophet, saying, Himself took our infirmities, and bare our sicknesses."

1 Peter 2:24 says, "Who his own self bare our sins in his own body on the tree, that we, being dead to sins, should live unto righteousness: by whose stripes ye were healed."

John 3:16 says, "For God so loved the world, that he gave his only begotten Son, that whosoever believeth in him should not perish, but have everlasting life."

Acts 9:34 says, "And Peter said unto him, Aeneas, Jesus Christ maketh thee **whole**: arise, and make thy bed. And he arose immediately."

The word (whole) and (ye were healed) are the same.

Hebrews 13:8 says, "Jesus Christ the same yesterday, and to day, and for ever."

There are things to consider in God's Word that can hinder God healing; Lack of faith, obedience (leper in Jordan seven times), your faith in agreement and walking right in the eyes of God and His Word.

Amos 3:3 says, "Can two walk together, except they be agreed?"

Matthew 18:19 says, "Again I say unto you, That if two of you shall agree on earth as touching any thing that they shall ask, it shall be done for them of my Father which is in heaven."

There are times that we confuse chastening of God with the devil himself.

Hebrews 12:6 says, "For whom the Lord loveth he chasteneth, and scourgeth every son whom he receiveth."

Chastening means, a) to punish in order to correct or make better; chastise. b) To restrain from excess; subdue. c) To make purer in style; refine

Matthew 7:9-11 says, "Or what man is there of you, whom if his son ask bread, will he give him a stone? For every one that asketh receiveth; and he that seeketh findeth; and to him that knocketh it shall be opened. Or what man is there of you, whom if his son ask bread, will he give him a stone? Or if he ask a fish, will he give him a serpent? If ye then, being evil, know how to give good gifts unto your children, how much more shall your Father which is in heaven give good things to them that ask him?"

<u>Healing Provided,</u>
Proverbs 4:20-22 says, "My son, attend to my words; incline thine ear unto my sayings. Let them not depart from thine eyes; keep them in the midst of thine heart. For they are life unto those that find them, and health to all their flesh."

John 1:1-3 says, "In the beginning was the Word, and the Word was with God, and the Word was God. The same was in the beginning with God. All things were made by him; and without him was not any thing made that was made."

John 1:14 says, "And the Word was made flesh, and dwelt among us, (and we beheld his glory, the glory as of the only begotten of the Father,) full of grace and truth."

John 10:10 says, "The thief cometh not, but for to steal, and to kill, and to destroy: I am come that they might have life, and that they might have it more abundantly."

2 Corinthians 5:21says, "For he hath made him to be sin for us, who knew no sin; that we might be made the righteousness of God in him."

Galatians 3:13 says, "Christ hath redeemed us from the curse of the law, being made a curse for us: for it is written, Cursed is every one that hangeth on a tree:"

Romans 6:23 says, "For the wages of sin is death; but the gift of God is eternal life through Jesus Christ our Lord."

John 17:17 says, "Sanctify them through thy truth: thy word is truth."
When it comes to healing, there are no impossibilities. Get these scriptures into your heart and don't let go. God is able to do exceeding and abundantly above that we could ever ask.

Romans 4:19-21 says, "And being not weak in faith, he considered not his own body now dead, when he was about an hundred years old, neither yet the deadness of Sara's womb: He staggered not at the promise of God through unbelief; but was strong in faith, giving glory to God; And being fully persuaded that, what he had promised, he was able also to perform."

Matthew 8:17 says, "That it might be fulfilled which was spoken by Esaias the prophet, saying, Himself took our infirmities, and bare our sicknesses."

Matthew 8:3 says, "And Jesus put forth his hand, and touched him, saying, I will; be thou clean. And immediately his leprosy was cleansed."

Romans 10:9 says, "That if thou shalt confess with thy mouth the Lord Jesus, and shalt believe in thine heart that God hath raised him from the dead, thou shalt be saved. For with the heart man believeth unto righteousness; and with the mouth confession is made unto salvation."

John 6:63 says, "It is the spirit that quickeneth; the flesh profiteth nothing: the words that I speak unto you, they are spirit, and they are life."

Psalms 107:20 says, "He sent his word, and healed them, and delivered them from their destructions."

Colossians 1:27 says, "To whom God would make known what is the riches of the glory of this mystery among the Gentiles; which is Christ in you, the hope of glory:"

One thing we know for sure is that God heals today. The reason for so much scripture is because God's Word is anointed. The Bible through the Holy Spirit is anointed more than any words we could give you. It is God's will for us to be healed. Healing is for these days we are living in. God does not put sickness upon us. Thanks to Jesus we have victory when it comes to healing.

Provision and the Love of Money

You do not have to have money to love it so much that it becomes sin. We know what it is like to need God's provision. This chapter is an obstacle that we need to apply to our lives.

When we think of provision....we usually think of money. Here we are talking about God providing all that we need. God's will is clear in His Word. As you read these verses there is going to be a release of the anointing to obtain all that you need. God's Word is anointed and will not turn back void.

Philippians 4:19 says, "But my God shall supply all your need according to his riches in glory by Christ Jesus."

3 John 1:2 says, "Beloved, I wish above all things that thou mayest prosper and be in health, even as thy soul prospereth."

Deuteronomy 28:11, 12 says, "And the Lord shall make thee plenteous in goods, in the fruit of thy body, and in the fruit of thy cattle, and in the fruit of thy ground, in the land which the Lord sware unto thy fathers to give thee. The Lord shall open unto thee his good treasure, the heaven to give the rain unto thy land in his season, and to bless all the work of thine hand: and thou shalt lend unto many nations, and thou shalt not borrow."

Deuteronomy 8:18 says, "But thou shalt remember the Lord thy God: for it is he that giveth thee power to get wealth, that he may establish his covenant which he sware unto thy fathers, as it is this day."

Proverbs 3:10 says, "So shall thy barns be filled with plenty, and thy presses shall burst out with new wine."

Ecclesiastes 5:19 says, "Every man also to whom God hath given riches and wealth, and hath given him power to eat thereof, and to take his portion, and to rejoice in his labour; this is the gift of God."

Provision means,
    a) A providing, preparing, or supplying of something. b) Something provided, prepared, or supplied for the future. c) A stock of food and other supplies assembled for future needs. d) A preparatory arrangement or measure taken in advance for meeting some future need. e) A clause, as in a legal document, agreement, etc., stipulating or requiring some specific thing; proviso; condition. f) Appointment to an office; esp., advance appointment by the pope to a see or benefice that is not yet vacant. g) To supply with provisions, esp. with a stock of food.

Romans 8:16, 17 says, "The Spirit itself beareth witness with our spirit, that we are the children of God: And if children, then heirs; heirs of God, and joint-heirs with Christ; if so be that we suffer with him, that we may be also glorified together."

Psalms 50:10-12 says, "For every beast of the forest is mine, and the cattle upon a thousand hills. I know all the fowls of the mountains: and the wild beasts of the field are mine. If I were hungry, I would not tell thee: for the world is mine, and the fulness thereof."

2 Chronicles 20:14-20 says, "Then upon Jahaziel the son Zechariah, the son of Benaiah, the son of Jeiel, the son of Mattaniah, a Levite of the sons of Asaph, came the Spirit of

the Lord in the midst of the congregation; And he said, Hearken ye, all Judah, and ye inhabitants of Jerusalem, and thou king Jehoshaphat, Thus saith the Lord unto you, Be not afraid nor dismayed by reason of this great multitude; for the battle is not yours, but God's. To morrow go ye down against them: behold, they come up by the cliff of Ziz; and ye shall find them at the end of the brook, before the wilderness of Jeruel. Ye shall not need to fight in this battle: set yourselves, stand ye still, and see the salvation of the Lord with you, O Judah and Jerusalem: fear not, nor be dismayed; to morrow go out against them: for the Lord will be with you. And Jehoshaphat bowed his head with his face to the ground: and all Judah and the inhabitants of Jerusalem fell before the Lord, worshipping the Lord. And the Levites, of the children of the Kohathites, and of the children of the Korhites, stood up to praise the Lord God of Israel with a loud voice on high. And they rose early in the morning, and went forth into the wilderness of Tekoa: and as they went forth, Jehoshaphat stood and said, Hear me, O Judah, and ye inhabitants of Jerusalem; Believe in the Lord your God, so shall ye be established; believe his prophets, so shall ye prosper."

Matthew 18:16 says, "But if he will not hear thee, then take with thee one or two more, that in the mouth of two or three witnesses every word may be established."

Matthew 6:20, 21 says, "But lay up for yourselves treasures in heaven, where neither moth nor rust doth corrupt, and where thieves do not break through nor steal: For where your treasure is, there will your heart be also."

Job 22:23-28 says, "If thou return to the Almighty, thou shalt be built up, thou shalt put away iniquity far from thy tabernacles. Then shalt thou lay up gold as dust, and the gold of Ophir as the stones of the brooks. Yea, the Almighty shall be thy defence, and thou shalt have plenty of silver. For then shalt thou have thy delight in the Almighty, and shalt lift up thy face unto God. Thou shalt make thy prayer unto him, and he shall hear thee, and thou shalt pay thy vows. Thou shalt also decree a thing, and it shall be established unto thee: and the light shall shine upon thy ways."

1 John 3:21-22 says, "Beloved, if our heart condemn us not, then have we confidence toward God. And whatsoever we ask, we receive of him, because we keep his commandments, and do those things that are pleasing in his sight."

Job 1:1 says, "There was a man in the land of Uz, whose name was Job; and **that man was perfect and upright, and one that feared God, and eschewed evil."**

We can learn a lesson from Job. Remember that God expects something from us, for His word to be applied to our lives. We are to be walking upright in the eyes of God.

John 1:3 says, "All things were made by him; and without him was not any thing made that was made."

John 21:6 says, "And he said unto them, Cast the net on the right side of the ship, and ye shall find. They cast therefore, and now they were not able to draw it for the multitude of fishes."
Jesus shows us here that He can and will provide more than enough.
Proverbs 3:10 says, "So shall thy barns be filled with plenty, and thy presses shall burst out with new wine."

Deuteronomy 28:11 says, "And the Lord shall make thee plenteous in goods, in the fruit of thy body, and in the fruit of thy cattle, and in the fruit of thy ground, in the land which the Lord sware unto thy fathers to give thee."

Deuteronomy 28:4-6 says, "Blessed shall be the fruit of thy body, and the fruit of thy ground, and the fruit of thy cattle, the increase of thy kine, and the flocks of thy sheep. Blessed shall be thy basket and thy store. Blessed shalt thou be when thou comest in, and blessed shalt thou be when thou goest out."

Deuteronomy 28:8 says, "The Lord shall command the blessing upon thee in thy storehouses, and in all that thou settest thine hand unto; and he shall bless thee in the land which the Lord thy God giveth thee."

Deuteronomy 28:11, 12 says, "And the Lord shall make thee plenteous in goods, in the fruit of thy body, and in the fruit of thy cattle, and in the fruit of thy ground, in the land which the Lord sware unto thy fathers to give thee. The Lord shall open unto thee his good treasure, the heaven to give the rain unto thy land in his season, and to bless all the work of thine hand: and thou shalt lend unto many nations, and thou shalt not borrow."

Use these scriptures to get the revelation of God our provider.

The Love of money is even more important. It is not when we have money that is not sin. Love of money is sin, (If we are trusting in the riches instead of trusting in God). According to some of these scriptures the love of money will keep us from Heaven.

Mark 10:17-24 says, "And when he was gone forth into the way, there came one running, and kneeled to him, and asked him, Good Master, what shall I do that I may inherit eternal life? And Jesus said unto him, Why callest thou me good? there is none good but one, that is, God. Thou knowest the commandments, Do not commit adultery, Do not kill, Do not steal, Do not bear false witness, Defraud not, Honour thy father and mother. And he answered and said unto him, Master, all these have I observed from my youth. Then Jesus beholding him loved him, and said unto him, One thing thou lackest: go thy way, sell whatsoever thou hast, and give to the poor, and thou shalt have treasure in heaven: and come, take up the cross, and follow me. And he was sad at that saying, and went away grieved: for he had great possessions. And Jesus looked round about, and saith unto his disciples, How hardly shall they that have riches enter into the kingdom of God! And the disciples were astonished at his words. But Jesus answereth again, and saith unto them, Children, how hard is it for them that trust in riches to enter into the kingdom of God!"

Matthew 6:32 says, "(For after all these things do the Gentiles seek:) for your heavenly Father knoweth that ye have need of all these things."

1 Corinthians 9:7 says, "Who goeth a warfare any time at his own charges? who planteth a vineyard, and eateth not of the fruit thereof? or who feedeth a flock, and eateth not of the milk of the flock?"

Everyone usually hates this part of anything to do with money. Tithe is the most important according to God's Word....To receive the provision of God.

Malachi 3:8, 9 says, "Will a man rob God? Yet ye have robbed me. But ye say, Wherein have we robbed thee? In tithes and offerings. Ye are cursed with a curse: for ye have robbed me, even this whole nation."

Leviticus 27:30 says, "And all the tithe of the land, whether of the seed of the land, or of the fruit of the tree, is the Lord's: it is holy unto the Lord."

Genesis 28:22 says, "And this stone, which I have set for a pillar, shall be God's house: and of all that thou shalt give me I will surely give the tenth unto thee."

1 Corinthians 9:11 says, "If we have sown unto you spiritual things, is it a great thing if we shall reap your carnal things?"

Malachi 3:10 says, "Bring ye all the tithes into the storehouse, that there may be meat in mine house, and prove me now herewith, saith the Lord of hosts, if I will not open you the windows of heaven, and pour you out a blessing, that there shall not be room enough to receive it."

God is our provider through prayer and walking upright in the sight of God. The love of money is the root of all evil. Bring the tithe into the storehouse (the Church you are a part of) The offerings goes to the Church. It should be ministries with fruit showing through their ministry.

Good and Bad Fears

Fear can become a monster.....but yet we go out or stay up late to watch scary movies. I remember when I was in the world (a sinner) the sicker the movie the better. Fear gives heart attacks, ulcers etc... There is good fear too....talking about the fear of God. These are extreme obstacles that need to be overcome. There is more with us than against us.

Ephesians 6:10-18 says, "Finally, my brethren, be strong in the Lord, and in the power of his might. Put on the whole armour of God, that ye may be able to stand against the wiles of the devil. For we wrestle not against flesh and blood, but against principalities, against powers, against the rulers of the darkness of this world, against spiritual wickedness in high places. Wherefore take unto you the whole armour of God, that ye may be able to withstand in the evil day, and having done all, to stand. Stand therefore, having your loins girt about with truth, and having on the breastplate of righteousness; And your feet shod with the preparation of the gospel of peace; Above all, taking the shield of faith, wherewith ye shall be able to quench all the fiery darts of the wicked. And take the helmet of salvation, and the sword of the Spirit, which is the word of God: Praying always with all prayer and supplication in the Spirit, and watching thereunto with all perseverance and supplication for all saints;"

First of all the bad fears come from wrong believing, if we are opening the door to doubts and fears. These things hinder the flow of God's power. These fears are of sin, Satan and this world. We need to resist them. Guard our hearts and minds. Fear can cause mental and physical torment.

Fear means, a) to be cowardly. b) A feeling of anxiety and agitation caused by the presence or nearness of danger, evil, pain, etc.; timidity; dread; terror; fright; apprehension. c) Respectful dread; awe; reverence. d) A feeling of uneasiness or apprehension; concern! a fear that it will rain." e) A cause for fear; possibility; chance! there was no fear of difficulty." f) to fill with fear; frighten. g) To be afraid of; dread. h) To feel reverence or awe for. I) To expect with misgiving; suspect! I fear I am late." j) to feel fear; be afraid. k) To be uneasy, anxious, or doubtful. l) For fear of in order to avoid or prevent; lest.

SYNONYM—fear is the general term for the anxiety and agitation felt at the presence of danger; dread refers to the fear or depression felt in anticipating something dangerous or disagreeable [to live in momentary fear [the mouse gave her a fright]; alarm implies the fright felt at the sudden realization of danger [he felt alarm at the sight of the pistol]; terror applies to an overwhelming, often paralyzing fear [the terror of soldiers in combat]; panic refers to a frantic, unreasoning fear, often one that spreads quickly and leads to irrational, aimless action [the cry of "fire!" created a panic]

If we are not able to face a problem....this is fear that we're dealing with. If we run from our problems instead of facing them, this results from lack of discipline and maturity. Fear of people or things, are based on lies of the devil. To get through an attack live in the truth of God's Word or being open to what God has for us. The truth will set us free.

On the other hand there is the fear of God that we all should have. This does not mean to be terrified of what God is going to do....but to be in awe and reverence for Him. This fear changes motives and entire lives from coming into the presence of the Lord. We shall see by faith our glorious majesties strength and power, His holiness, mercy and love. We need to come to the realization that He and He alone is the source, the supplier of everything now and forever.

There are great rewards for Godly fear. It is the beginning of wisdom. It is the knowledge of a fountain of life.

Psalms 34:9 says, "O fear the Lord, ye his saints: for there is no want to them that fear him."

Psalms 145:19 says, "He will fulfil the desire of them that fear him: he also will hear their cry, and will save them. The Lord **preserveth** all them that love him: but all the wicked will he destroy."

Preserveth means, Taking pleasure.

Psalms 34:7 says, "The angel of the Lord encampeth round about them that fear him, and delivereth them."

1 John 4:18 says, "There is no fear in love; but perfect love casteth out fear: because fear hath torment. He that feareth is not made perfect in love."

Psalms 34:4 says, "I sought the Lord, and he heard me, and delivered me from all my fears." (This is talking about worldly fears.)

Right believing calms the spirit and connects us with God's mighty power. God's power delivers us from any and all obstacles.

2 Timothy 1:7 says, "For God hath not given us the spirit of fear; but of power, and of love, and of a sound mind."

Isaiah 41:10 says, "Fear thou not; for I am with thee: be not dismayed; for I am thy God: I will strengthen thee; yea, I will help thee; yea, I will uphold thee with the right hand of my righteousness."

Psalms 27:1 says, "The Lord is my light and my salvation; whom shall I fear? the Lord is the strength of my life; of whom shall I be afraid?"

Psalms 23:4 says, "Yea, though I walk through the valley of the shadow of death, I will fear no evil: for thou art with me; thy rod and thy staff they comfort me."

Psalms 56:11 says, "In God have I put my trust: I will not be afraid what man can do unto me."

Psalms 91:1-16 says, "He that dwelleth in the secret place of the most High shall abide under the shadow of the Almighty. I will say of the Lord, He is my refuge and my fortress: my God; in him will I trust. Surely he shall deliver thee from the snare of the fowler, and from the noisome pestilence. He shall cover thee with his feathers, and under his wings shalt thou trust: his truth shall be thy shield and buckler. Thou shalt not be afraid for the terror by night; nor for the arrow that flieth by day; Nor for the pestilence that walketh in darkness; nor for the destruction that wasteth at noonday. A thousand shall fall at thy side, and ten thousand at thy right hand; but it shall not come nigh thee. Only with thine eyes shalt thou behold and see the reward of the wicked. Because thou hast made the Lord, which is my refuge, even the most High, thy habitation; There shall no evil befall thee, neither shall any plague come nigh thy dwelling. For he shall give his angels charge over thee, to keep thee in all thy ways. They shall bear thee up in their hands, lest thou dash thy foot against a stone. Thou shalt tread upon the lion and adder: the young lion and the dragon shalt thou trample under feet. Because he hath set his love upon me, therefore will I deliver him: I will set him on high, because he hath known my name. He shall call upon me, and I will answer him: I will be with him in trouble; I will deliver him, and honour him. With long life will I satisfy him, and shew him my salvation."

Psalms 121:1-8 says, "I Will lift up mine eyes unto the hills, from whence cometh my help. My help cometh from the Lord, which made heaven and earth. He will not suffer thy foot to be moved: he that keepeth thee will not slumber. Behold, he that keepeth Israel shall neither slumber nor sleep. The Lord is thy keeper: the Lord is thy shade upon thy right hand. The sun shall not smite thee by day, nor the moon by night. The Lord shall preserve thee from all evil: he shall preserve thy soul. The Lord shall preserve thy going out and thy coming in from this time forth, and even for evermore."

The fear of the Lord is to hate evil.

Proverbs 8:13 says, "The fear of the Lord is to hate evil: pride, and arrogancy, and the evil way, and the froward mouth, do I hate."

There is a fear that God will not tolerate.....Fear of taking a stand for Him. To be ashamed of God makes Him ashamed of us. This is as good as an unforgiving sinner.

Revelation 21:8 says, "But the fearful, and unbelieving, and abominable, and murderers, and whoremongers, and sorcerers, and idolaters, and all liars, shall have their part in the lake which burneth with fire and brimstone: which is the second death."

Matthew 10:33 says, "But whosoever shall deny me before men, him will I also deny before my Father which is in heaven."

Malachi 3:16, 17 says, "Then they that feared the Lord spake often one to another: and the Lord hearkened, and heard it, and a book of remembrance was written before him for them that feared the Lord, and that thought upon his name. And they shall be mine, saith the Lord of hosts, in that day when I make up my jewels; and I will spare them, as a man spareth his own son that serveth him."

To overcome all fears.....a change of our lives is a must. Remember to have a problem with fear (good and bad) can be the difference from Heaven and Hell. Be in fear of God all day and every day. Become out spoken about our lives as Christians.

God is a Comforting God

On the topic of comfort, we want you to completely understand. God wants to fill that void in our lives. Comfort us in the bad times. Thinking that God doesn't care enough to comfort us, is the obstacle to overcome.

Hebrews 13:5 says, "Let your conversation be without covetousness; and be content with such things as ye have: for he hath said, I will never leave thee, nor forsake thee."

Psalms 27:10 says, "When my father and my mother forsake me, then the Lord will take me up."

Matthew 11:28 says, "Come unto me, all ye that labour and are heavy laden, and I will give you rest."

2 Corinthians 1:3, 4 says, "Blessed be God, even the Father of our Lord Jesus Christ, the Father of mercies, and the God of all comfort; Who comforteth us in all our tribulation, that we may be able to comfort them which are in any trouble, by the comfort wherewith we ourselves are comforted of God."

Psalms 119:49, 50 says, "Remember the word unto thy servant, upon which thou hast caused me to hope. This is my comfort in my affliction: for thy word hath quickened me."

Isaiah 61:1 says, "The Spirit of the Lord God is upon me; because the Lord hath anointed me to preach good tidings unto the meek; he hath sent me to bind up the brokenhearted, to proclaim liberty to the captives, and the opening of the prison to them that are bound;"

God will comfort you, because He cares. You can comfort others because, Christ is within you.

John 14:16 says, "And I will pray the Father, and he shall give you another Comforter, that he may abide with you for ever;"

There are many things that affect us, to the point of needing comforted. The effect may come from, a loss of loved one or even losing a job. We may have a situation on our job that bothers us. Everyone faces rejection at some time, depression or sadness for any reason. Children growing up may get made fun of. (God is here for us today and forever.)

1 Thessalonians 4:13 says, "But I would not have you to be ignorant, brethren, concerning them which are asleep, that ye sorrow not, even as others which have no hope."

2 Corinthians 5:6-8 says, "Therefore we are always confident, knowing that, whilst we are at home in the body, we are absent from the Lord: (For we walk by faith, not by sight:) We are confident, I say, and willing rather to be absent from the body, and to be present with the Lord."

Revelation 21:4 says, "And God shall wipe away all tears from their eyes; and there shall be no more death, neither sorrow, nor crying, neither shall there be any more pain: for the former things are passed away."

Psalms 23:4 says, "Yea, though I walk through the valley of the shadow of death, I will fear no evil: for thou art with me; thy rod and thy staff they comfort me."

He will never leave you nor forsake you.

Matthew 5:4 says, "Blessed are they that mourn: for they shall be comforted."

Remember God is there for you. When Life at times seems hard, just knowing this fact can help you. Remember if you are saved.....having asked Jesus into your heart. You can be assured that greater is He

(JESUS) that is in you, than he (Satan) that is in the world.

Abominable Things

God hates all sin. We believe that there are certain things worse than others. This chapter is about, those things that are detestable things.....hateful to God.

Abominable means,
a) Nasty and disgusting; vile; loathsome. b) Highly unpleasant; disagreeable; very bad! Abominable taste

SYNONYM: HATEFUL
Deuteronomy 7:25 says, "The graven images of their gods shall ye burn with fire: thou shalt not desire the silver or gold that is on them, nor take it unto thee, lest thou be snared therein: for it is an abomination to the Lord thy God."

Deuteronomy 18:10-12 says, "There shall not be found among you any one that maketh his son or his daughter to pass through the fire, or that useth divination, or an observer of times, or an enchanter, or a witch. Or a charmer, or a consulter with familiar spirits, or a wizard, or a necromancer. For all that do these things are an abomination unto the Lord: and because of these abominations the Lord thy God doth drive them out from before thee."

Deuteronomy 25:16 says, "For all that do such things, and all that do unrighteously, are an abomination unto the Lord thy God."

Proverbs 6:12-16 says, "A naughty person, a wicked man, walketh with a froward mouth. He winketh with his eyes, he speaketh with his feet, he teacheth with his fingers; Frowardness is in his heart, he deviseth mischief continually; he soweth discord. Therefore shall his calamity come suddenly; suddenly shall he be broken without remedy.

These six things doth the Lord hate: yea, seven are an abomination unto him:"

Proverbs 11:20 says, "They that are of a froward heart are abomination to the Lord: but such as are upright in their way are his delight."

Proverbs 12:22 says, "Lying lips are abomination to the Lord: but they that deal truly are his delight."

Proverbs 21:27 says, "The sacrifice of the wicked is abomination: how much more, when he bringeth it with a wicked mind?"

Proverbs 28:9 says, "He that turneth away his ear from hearing the law, even his prayer shall be abomination."

Luke 16:15 says, "And he said unto them, Ye are they which justify yourselves before men; but God knoweth your hearts: for that which is highly esteemed among men is abomination in the sight of God."

We are teachers; it is our responsibility to give you the whole truth. This may be hard to consider, being any abomination to God. Don't let pride get between you and repentance if needed. At this time search your heart and pray. Seek the Lord and cleanse yourself from any abomination.

Getting Out of the Rut

Have you ever felt like you were not moving anywhere in life? Do you feel that you're not growing spiritually? Everyone seems to get ahead and you just stay in one place all the time. I was in this place a while back, and God rescued me.

Rut means,
a) A groove, furrow, or track, esp. one made in the ground by the passage of wheeled vehicles. b) A fixed, routine course of action, thought, etc., esp. one regarded as dull and unrewarding.

God Shows in this illustration that we need help sometimes. If you drive a car in the rain, on a dirt road.....there is a good chance you'll get stuck. If you get stuck and try to get out yourself, you probably will get deeper and deeper. It's time to call the tow truck. This is a good example of Christians. Problems come and we try to fix them by ourselves. We don't get any where until we call on God.

You may be in a rut right now, not knowing what to do. God will never leave you nor forsake you.

3 John 1:2 says, "Beloved, I wish above all things that thou mayest prosper and be in health, even as thy soul prospereth."
Which road will you choose? The narrow road is to God. Going to fast you might get stuck. Going to slow you might get hit and in a rut. If you're not moving at all, you're just stuck. The perfect speed is moving with God. The road in life is not perfect but it is narrow. We stay in God's will, we will keep moving ahead.

Mindset and Limitations

The Word of God says that, where there is no vision the people perish. Sometimes as Christians we set a small vision for our future. We have a big God and He is able to do more than we can even think. Learning to overcome mindsets and/or limitations is what this chapter is about.

Isaiah 54:2, 3 says, "Enlarge the place of thy tent, and let them stretch forth the curtains of thine habitations: spare not, lengthen thy cords, and strengthen thy stakes; For thou shalt break forth on the right hand and on the left; and thy seed shall inherit the Gentiles, and make the desolate cities to be inhabited."

Jeremiah 32:17 says, "Ah Lord God! behold, thou hast made the heaven and the earth by thy great power and stretched out arm, and there is nothing too hard for thee:"

Jeremiah 32:27 says, "Behold, I am the Lord, the God of all flesh: is there any thing too hard for me?"

Hosea 12:10 says, "I have also spoken by the prophets, and I have multiplied visions, and used similitudes, by the ministry of the prophets."

God spoke to a church that they were going to seat one thousand people. After a few years they said that what God spoke was past. They believed that God more or less changed His mind. They gave up on the big vision of God.

Sometime we believe that the saints give up on the brink of a miracle.

Philippians 4:13 says, "I can do all things through Christ which strengtheneth me."

Philippians 4:19 says, "But my God shall supply all your need according to his riches in glory by Christ Jesus."

James 4:1-8 says, "From whence come wars and fightings among you? come they not hence, even of your lusts that war in your members? Ye lust, and have not: ye kill, and desire to have, and cannot obtain: ye fight and war, yet ye have not, because ye ask not. Ye ask, and receive not, because ye ask amiss, that ye may consume it upon your lusts. Ye adulterers and adulteresses, know ye not that the friendship of the world is enmity with God? whosoever therefore will be a friend of the world is the enemy of God. Do ye think that the scripture saith in vain, The spirit that dwelleth in us lusteth to envy? But he giveth more grace. Wherefore he saith, God resisteth the proud, but giveth grace unto the humble. Submit yourselves therefore to God. Resist the devil, and he will flee from you. Draw nigh to God, and he will draw nigh to you. Cleanse your hands, ye sinners; and purify your hearts, ye double minded."

At this time in your life remember God's time is best.

Recently I was ministering to a woman. God said that He hadn't forgotten about business that she was to have, but it wasn't time yet. This woman was encouraged because the hope was getting slim. God knows where we are, what we need. God knows us every minute of every day. Hold on and don't let go.

God Will Help Us
Where does our help come from? (God)

Deuteronomy 33:29 says, "Happy art thou, O Israel: who is like unto thee, O people saved by the Lord, the shield of thy help, and who is the sword of thy excellency! and thine enemies shall be found liars unto thee; and thou shalt tread upon their high places."

2 Chronicles 25:8 says, "But if thou wilt go, do it; be strong for the battle: God shall make thee fall before the enemy: for God hath power to help, and to cast down."

Psalms 27:9 says, "Hide not thy face far from me; put not thy servant away in anger: thou hast been my help; leave me not, neither forsake me, O God of my salvation."

Psalms 28:7 says, "The Lord is my strength and my shield; my heart trusted in him, and I am helped: therefore my heart greatly rejoiceth; and with my song will I praise him."

Psalms 40:17 says, "But I am poor and needy; yet the Lord thinketh upon me: thou art my help and my deliverer; make no tarrying, O my God."

Isaiah 41:10 says, "Fear thou not; for I am with thee: be not dismayed; for I am thy God: I will strengthen thee; yea, I will help thee; yea, I will uphold thee with the right hand of my righteousness."
Isaiah 50:9 says, "Behold, the Lord God will help me; who is he that shall condemn me? lo, they all shall wax old as a garment; the moth shall eat them up."

Hebrews 13:6 says, "So that we may boldly say, The Lord is my helper, and I will not fear what man shall do unto me."

Exodus 14:16 says, "But lift thou up thy rod, and stretch out thine hand over the sea, and divide it: and the children of Israel shall go on dry ground through the midst of the sea."

James 3:17 says, "But the wisdom that is from above is first pure, then peaceable, gentle, and easy to be intreated, full of mercy and good fruits, without partiality, and without hypocrisy."

Proverbs 15:19 says, "The way of the slothful man is as an hedge of thorns: but the way of the righteous is made plain."

Isaiah 30:21says, "And thine ears shall hear a word behind thee, saying, This is the way, walk ye in it, when ye turn to the right hand, and when ye turn to the left."

Isaiah 42:16 says, "And I will bring the blind by a way that they knew not; I will lead them in paths that they have not known: I will make darkness light before them, and crooked things straight. These things will I do unto them, and not forsake them."

Every time that we've ever needed help, God was there. We ask this Question all the time.....If Jesus was right here right now.....and would go where you go.....would you go? Would you walk in Evangelism? How about praying for the sick while preaching to the poor? Jesus is with you and He will never leave you. This chapter's verses should be read over and over again.

New Days Ahead

We as of right now, are in what we call a time of renewal, when God visits us through His Holy Spirit. This topic of new days ahead can be a huge obstacle. God does not change but yet we believe that He is doing a new thing. It doesn't matter what it looks like.....God is moving.

Job 1:1 says, "There was a man in the land of Uz, whose name was Job; and that man was perfect and upright, and one that feared God, and eschewed evil."

James 5:11says, "Behold, we count them happy which endure. Ye have heard of the patience of Job, and have seen the end of the Lord; that the Lord is very pitiful, and of tender mercy."

A patient man
Job 1:13-17 says, "And there was a day when his sons and his daughters were eating and drinking wine in their eldest brother's house: And there came a messenger unto Job, and said, The oxen were plowing, and the asses feeding beside them: And the Sabeans fell upon them, and took them away; yea, they have slain the servants with the edge of the sword; and I only am escaped alone to tell thee. While he was yet speaking, there came also another, and said, The fire of God is fallen from heaven, and hath burned up the sheep, and the servants, and consumed them; and I only am escaped alone to tell thee. While he was yet speaking, there came also another, and said, The Chaldeans made out three bands, and fell upon the camels, and have carried them away, yea, and slain the servants with the edge of the sword; and I only am escaped alone to tell thee."

Lost his property
Job 1:18, 19 says, "While he was yet speaking, there came also another, and said, Thy sons and thy daughters were eating and drinking wine in their eldest brother's house: And, behold, there came a great wind from the wilderness, and smote the four corners of the house, and it fell upon the young men, and they are dead; and I only am escaped alone to tell thee."

Lost his children
Job 1:20-22 says, "Then Job arose, and rent his mantle, and shaved his head, and fell down upon the ground, and worshipped, And said, Naked came I out of my mother's womb, and naked shall I return thither: the Lord gave, and the Lord hath taken away; blessed be the name of the Lord. In all this Job sinned not, nor charged God foolishly."

Job sinned not
Job 2:7-9 says, "So went Satan forth from the presence of the Lord, and smote Job with sore boils from the sole of his foot unto his crown. And he took him a potsherd to scrape himself withal; and he sat down among the ashes. Then said his wife unto him, Dost thou still retain thine integrity? curse God, and die."

He lost his health and those who are closest to us will try to get us to turn on God.

Job still sinned not
Job 16:1-3 says, "Then Job answered and said, I have heard many such things: miserable comforters are ye all. Shall vain words have an end? or what emboldeneth thee that thou answerest?"

Job had a lack of sympathy for his self.
Job 30:10 says, "They abhor me, they flee far from me, and spare not to spit in my face."

Job lost friends
Job 19:7-20 says, "Behold, I cry out of wrong, but I am not heard: I cry aloud, but there is no judgment. He hath fenced up my way that I cannot pass, and he hath set darkness in my paths. He hath stripped me of my glory, and taken the crown from my head. He hath destroyed me on every side, and I am gone: and mine hope hath he removed like a tree. He hath also kindled his wrath against me, and he counteth me unto him as one of his enemies. His troops come together, and raise up their way against me, and encamp round about my tabernacle. He hath put my brethren far from me, and mine acquaintance are verily estranged from me. My kinsfolk have failed, and my familiar friends have forgotten me. They that dwell in mine house, and my maids, count me for a stranger: I am an alien in their sight. I called my servant, and he gave me no answer; I intreated him with my mouth. My breath is strange to my wife, though I intreated for the children's sake of mine own body. Yea, young children despised me; I arose, and they spake against me. All my inward friends abhorred me: and they whom I loved are turned against me. My bone cleaveth to my skin and to my flesh, and I am escaped with the skin of my teeth."

Faith was very strained but in the end, Job was victoriously delivered.

Job 42:10 says, "And the Lord turned the captivity of Job, when he prayed for his friends: also the Lord gave Job twice as much as he had before."

Job 42:11 says, "Then came there unto him all his brethren, and all his sisters, and all they that had been of his acquaintance before, and did eat bread with him in his house: and they bemoaned him, and comforted him over all the evil that the Lord had brought upon him: every man also gave him a piece of money, and every one an earring of gold."

Job 42:16, 17 says, "After this lived Job an hundred and forty years, and saw his sons, and his sons' sons, even four generations. So Job died, being old and full of days."

Jesus is the same yesterday, today and forever. God's Word also says that He is able to do exceedingly, abundantly, above all that we could ask or think. Jesus will never leave you nor forsake you.

We could all learn from the life of Job. Understand that we don't know what is ahead. God has a plan. Job was perfect, upright and patient. Job lost his property and children. Job became ill with sores and boils. His wife spoke awful to him. His friends turned against him. Job's faith was almost gone.

There are new days ahead for you........God is moving more and more. If you have faced allot of hard times payday is coming.

Discovering Our Purpose

We all have a purpose on this Earth. God has a special plan for you and me. This is the greatest time since the world began. God is going to pour out His Spirit upon all flesh. This is another obstacle that we need to overcome.

The Angel came to Mary and told her, she would be giving birth to a son. (Jesus)

Matthew 1:20-25 says, "But while he thought on these things, behold, the angel of the Lord appeared unto him in a dream, saying, Joseph, thou son of David, fear not to take unto thee Mary thy wife: for that which is conceived in her is of the Holy Ghost. And she shall bring forth a son, and thou shalt call his name JESUS: for he shall save his people from their sins. Now all this was done, that it might be fulfilled which was spoken of the Lord by the prophet, saying, Behold, a virgin shall be with child, and shall bring forth a son, and they shall call his name Emmanuel, which being interpreted is, God with us. Then Joseph being raised from sleep did as the angel of the Lord had bidden him, and took unto him his wife: And knew her not till she had brought forth her firstborn son: and he called his name JESUS."

Jeremiah 32:27 says, "Behold, I am the Lord, the God of all flesh: is there any thing too hard for me?"

Jesus was born for a purpose, to save us from sin. When God does something, there is usually a purpose.

1 Peter 2:24 says, "Who his own self bare our sins in his own body on the tree, that we, being dead to sins, should live unto righteousness: by whose stripes ye were healed."

God spoke something and about one year later, it came to pass. God said that I would be a teacher before my time. I have had multiple opportunities to teach.

1 Corinthians 15:57, 58 says, "But thanks be to God, which giveth us the victory through our Lord Jesus Christ. Therefore, my beloved brethren, be ye stedfast, unmoveable, always abounding in the work of the Lord, forasmuch as ye know that your labour is not in vain in the Lord."

Hebrews 13:20, 21 says, "Now the God of peace, that brought again from the dead our Lord Jesus, that great shepherd of the sheep, through the blood of the everlasting covenant, Make you perfect in every good work to do his will, working in you that which is well pleasing in his sight, through Jesus Christ; to whom be glory for ever and ever. Amen."

3 John 1:2 says, "Beloved, I wish above all things that thou mayest prosper and be in health, even as thy soul prospereth."

Romans 8:28-31 says, "And we know that all things work together for good to them that love God, to them who are the called according to his purpose. For whom he did foreknow, he also did predestinate to be conformed to the image of his Son, that he might be the firstborn among many brethren. Moreover whom he did predestinate, them he also called: and whom he called, them he also justified: and whom he justified, them he also glorified. What shall we then say to these things? If God be for us, who can be against us?"

Hebrews 10:23 says, "Let us hold fast the profession of our faith without wavering; (for he is faithful that promised ;)"

Hebrews 10:35-38 says, "Cast not away therefore your confidence, which hath great recompence of reward. For ye have need of patience, that, after ye have done the will of

God, ye might receive the promise. For yet a little while, and he that shall come will come, and will not tarry. Now the just shall live by faith: but if any man draws back, my soul shall have no pleasure in him."

Faith comes by hearing and hearing by the Word of God.

Ephesians 3:11 says, "According to the eternal purpose which he purposed in Christ Jesus our Lord:"

Proverbs 29:18 says, "Where there is no vision, the people perish: but he that keepeth the law, happy is he."

Proverbs 13:12 says, "Hope deferred maketh the heart sick: but when the desire cometh, it is a tree of life."

Proverbs 21:5 says, "The thoughts of the diligent tend only to plenteousness; but of every one that is hasty only to want."

Proverbs 16:3 says, "Commit thy works unto the Lord, and thy thoughts shall be established."

Proverbs 4:6-14 says, "Forsake her not, and she shall preserve thee: love her, and she shall keep thee. Wisdom is the principal thing; therefore get wisdom: and with all thy getting get understanding. Exalt her, and she shall promote thee: she shall bring thee to honour, when thou dost embrace her. She shall give to thine head an ornament of grace: a crown of glory shall she deliver to thee. Hear, O my son, and receive my sayings; and the years of thy life shall be many. I have taught thee in the way of wisdom; I have led thee in right paths. When thou goest, thy steps shall not be straitened; and when thou runnest, thou shalt not stumble. Take fast hold of instruction; let her not go: keep her; for she is thy life. Enter not into the path of the wicked, and go not in the way of evil men."

The Angel spoke to Mary and God did what he said. Moses and Mary had a great purpose. There is a purpose for you. No matter what it looks like. There is a purpose and God will shine upon it guaranteed.

Removing the Obstacle

Repentance will be needed to overcome obstacles. If there has been anything in your life that needs to be overcome.....this chapter is for you. God overcame Satan and threw him out of Heaven. Jesus overcame temptation and also death through His resurrection. We can overcome any sin or obstacle as sons and daughters of God.

Deuteronomy 1:21says, "Behold, the Lord thy God hath set the land before thee: go up and possess it, as the Lord God of thy fathers hath said unto thee; fear not, neither be discouraged."
Possess means, to own or obtain.

Joshua 1:9 says, "Have not I commanded thee? Be strong and of a good courage; be not afraid, neither be thou dismayed: for the Lord thy God is with thee whithersoever thou goest."

God will never leave you nor forsake you.

Synonyms of Dismayed are; Disturb, bother, scare, discourage and confuse.

2 Chronicles 20:15-17 says, "And he said, Hearken ye, all Judah, and ye inhabitants of Jerusalem, and thou king Jehoshaphat, Thus saith the Lord unto you, Be not afraid nor dismayed by reason of this great multitude; for the battle is not yours, but God's. To morrow go ye down against them: behold, they come up by the cliff of Ziz; and ye shall find them at the end of the brook, before the wilderness of Jeruel. Ye shall not need to fight in this battle: set yourselves, stand ye still, and see the salvation of the Lord with you, O Judah

and Jerusalem: fear not, nor be dismayed; to morrow go out against them: for the Lord will be with you."

The battle is not your but mine saith the Lord.

Synonyms for battle are; Strife, struggle, conflict and warfare.

Psalms 107:19, 20 says, "Then they cry unto the Lord in their trouble, and he saveth them out of their distresses. He sent his word, and healed them, and delivered them from their destructions."

God healed them and saved them.
Synonyms for distresses are; Torment, misery, torture and disaster.

Philippians 4:13 says, "I can do all things through Christ which strengtheneth me." The things from the past we have to forget. Many times the past life will bring discouragement...

Past means, a) Gone or finished. b) Gone over.

Isaiah 54:17 says, "**No weapon that is formed against thee shall prosper**; and every tongue that shall rise against thee in judgment thou shalt condemn. This is the heritage of the servants of the Lord, and their righteousness is of me, saith the Lord."

Synonyms for prosper are; Succeed, win and prevail.

God will never leave us, He will never forsake us. God will fight our battles for us. God saves us from our troubles. God heals and forgets the past.

Isaiah 40:4 says, "Every valley shall be exalted, and every mountain and hill shall be made low: and the crooked shall be made straight, and the rough places plain."

Isaiah 45:2 says, "I will go before thee, and make the crooked places straight: I will break in pieces the gates of brass, and cut in sunder the bars of iron."

Zechariah 4:7 says, "Who art thou, O great mountain? before Zerubbabel thou shalt become a plain: and he shall bring forth the headstone thereof with shoutings, crying, Grace, grace unto it."

Matthew 22:21 says, "They say unto him, Caesar's. Then saith he unto them, Render therefore unto Caesar the things which are Caesar's; and unto God the things that are God's."

Isaiah 57:15 says, "For thus saith the high and lofty One that inhabiteth eternity, whose name is Holy; I dwell in the high and holy place, with him also that is of a contrite and humble spirit, to revive the spirit of the humble, and to revive the heart of the contrite ones."

An obstacle is something that stands in the way. Remember, we are over comers. It doesn't matter where you've been.....God loves you and we are able to overcome anything through Christ. The prayer of Salvation Salvation is the purpose for us. Jesus died for all of us. Here is a prayer that has all the details that should be. You can use this prayer. Memorize the prayer so you can be ready to lead someone to Jesus.

Dear Jesus, I believe that you are the son of God and that you died for me and arose again on the third day. Have mercy on me. I Acknowledge and repent for my transgressions, for it was against thee that I sinned. I am truly sorry and I claim the blood for the cleansing of my iniquity. Create in me a clean heart and renew a right spirit within me. Help me to be an over comer never again to follow the enticements of the devil. Please come into my heart this day, I sincerely want to be thy child. Thank you Jesus for saving me Amen! (I want you

to truly understanding that Jesus died and arose again for our sin.)

Recommended Books

By Bill Vincent

Overcoming Obstacles
Glory: Pursuing God's Presence
Defeating the Demonic Realm
Increasing Your Prophetic Gift
Increase Your Anointing
Keys to Receiving Your Miracle
The Supernatural Realm
Waves of Revival
Increase of Revelation and Restoration
The Resurrection Power of God
Discerning Your Call of God
Apostolic Breakthrough
Glory: Increasing God's Presence
Love is Waiting – Don't Let Love Pass You By
The Healing Power of God
Glory: Expanding God's Presence
Receiving Personal Prophecy
Signs and Wonders
Signs and Wonders Revelations
Children Stories
The Rapture
The Secret Place of God's Power
Building a Prototype Church
Breakthrough of Spiritual Strongholds
Glory: Revival Presence of God
Overcoming the Power of Lust
Glory: Kingdom Presence of God
Transitioning to the Prototype Church
The Stronghold of Jezebel
Healing After Divorce
A Closer Relationship With God
Cover Up and Save Yourself

Desperate for God's Presence
The War for Spiritual Battles
Spiritual Leadership
Global Warning
Millions of Churches
Destroying the Jezebel Spirit
Awakening of Miracles
Deception and Consequences Revealed
Are You a Follower of Christ
Don't Let the Enemy Steal from You!
A Godly Shaking
The Unsearchable Riches of Christ
Heaven's Court System
Satan's Open Doors
Armed for Battle
The Wrestler
Spiritual Warfare: Complete Collection
Growing In the Prophetic
Faith
The Angry Fighter's Story
Understanding Heaven's Court System

Web Site:
www.revivalwavesofgloryministries.com

www.ingramcontent.com/pod-product-compliance
Lightning Source LLC
Chambersburg PA
CBHW052059070526
44584CB00017B/2249